THE SEARCH FOR COMMUNITY IN MODERN AMERICA

EDITED BY

E. DIGBY BALTZELL

University of Pennsylvania

HARPER & ROW, PUBLISHERS
NEW YORK, EVANSTON, AND LONDON

THE SEARCH FOR COMMUNITY IN MODERN AMERICA

Copyright © 1968 by E. Digby Baltzell
Printed in the United States of America. All rights reserved. No part of this book may be used or reproduced in any manner whatsoever without written permission except in the case of brief quotations embodied in critical articles and reviews. For information address Harper & Row, Publishers, Incorporated, 49 East 33rd Street, New York, N.Y. 10016.

Library of Congress Catalog Card Number: 68-12924

THE SEARCH FOR COMMUNITY IN MODERN AMERICA

INTERPRETATIONS OF AMERICAN HISTORY

JOHN HIGHAM AND BRADFORD PERKINS, EDITORS

CONTENTS

EDITORS' INTRODUCTION

This volume—and companions in the series, "Interpretations of American History"—makes a special effort to cope with one of the basic dilemmas confronting every student of history. On the one hand, historical knowledge shares a characteristic common to all appraisals of human affairs. It is partial and selective. It picks out some features and facts of a situation while ignoring others that may be equally pertinent. The more selective an interpretation is, the more memorable and widely applicable it can be. On the other hand, history has to provide what nothing else does: a total estimate, a multifaceted synthesis, of man's experience in particular times and places. To study history, therefore, is to strive simultaneously for a clear, selective focus and for an integrated, over-all view.

In that spirit, each book of the series aims to resolve the varied literature on a major topic or event into a meaningful whole. One interpretation, we believe, does not deserve as much of a student's attention as another simply because they are in conflict. Instead of contriving a balance between opposing views, or choosing polemical material simply to create an appearance of controversy, Professor Baltzell has exercised his own judgment on the relative importance of different aspects or interpretations of a problem. We have asked him to select some of what he considers the best, most persuasive writings bearing on the search for community in modern America, indicating in the introductory essay and headnotes his reasons for considering these accounts convincing or significant. When appropriate, he has also brought out the relation between older and more recent approaches to the subject. The editor's own competence and experience in the field enable him to provide a sense of order and to indicate the evolution and complexity of interpretations. He is, then, like other editors in this series, an informed participant rather than a mere observer, a student sharing with other students the results of his own investigations of the literature on a crucial phase of American development.

JOHN HIGHAM
BRADFORD PERKINS

THE SEARCH FOR COMMUNITY IN MODERN AMERICA

INTRODUCTION

History's lessons but record
One death-grapple in the darkness
'Twixt old systems and the Word.
JAMES RUSSELL LOWELL

None of us is primarily interested in abstractions; we become so only because they often help us to understand unique and concrete events and issues. After teaching a wide variety of students at a large urban university for some years, one has the impression that majors in the social sciences are too often burdened with abstract concepts (or analytical points of view) without much knowledge of past or present events; history majors, on the other hand, do know some history but often lack a conceptual point of view with which to organize their knowledge in some meaningful way. In this brief book, therefore, an attempt has been made to include essays which deal rather concretely with various aspects of a central theoretical issue—the nature of community cohesion. Although the essays cover many areas of American life in the twentieth century—with constant references to their historical backgrounds—they are held together, one would hope, by a consistent point of view rather than by any chronological order. Finally, while all the essays refer to American society, it is well to bear in mind that the search for new forms of community is of more general concern, affecting all of Western society in the nineteenth and twentieth centuries, as well as the developing nations in Asia, Africa, and South America, today, and increasingly so in the future.

I

Coming home from a night job in the early hours of a March morning in 1964, a young lady, Catherine Genovese, was stabbed repeatedly and over an extended period of time. Thirty-eight fellow residents of Kew Gardens, a respectable New York City neighborhood, admitted to having witnessed at least part of the attack. None of them, however, went to her aid, nor did anyone call the police until after she was dead. The crime, or rather the lack of community response to it, produced a sense of indignation and frustration which spread across the nation. Senator Richard Russell of Georgia read *The New York Times* account of it into the *Congressional Record,* and the Law School of The University of Chicago eventually sponsored a "Conference on the Good Samaritan and the Bad—The Law and Morality of Volunteering in Situations of Peril, or of Failing to Do So." The "Genovese case," and especially the wide and overly emotional discussions of it in the mass media, served to dramatize the problem of community cohesion in modern society.

The concept of community is often used, but less often defined Perhaps the following definition will be helpful; it was set forth by Robert A. Nisbet in an exhaustive treatment of the classic sociological discussions of the problem:

> By community [he wrote], I mean something that goes far beyond mere local community. The word as we find it in much nineteenth- and twentieth-century thought encompasses all forms of relationships which are characterized by a high degree of personal intimacy, emotional depth, moral commitment, social cohesion, and continuity in time. Community is founded on man conceived in his wholeness rather than in one or another of the roles, taken separately, that he may hold in the social order. It draws its psychological strength from levels of motivation deeper than those of mere volition or interest, and it achieves its fulfillment in a submergence of individual will that is not possible in unions of mere convenience or rational assent. Community is a fusion of feeling and thought, of tradition and commitment, of membership and volition. It may be found in, or given symbolic expression by, locality, religion, nation, race, occupation, or crusade.

The gradual erosion, in modern society, of the traditional community ties which Professor Nisbet describes is both the cause and the result of extensive social mobility, individuation, anonymity, and the consequent prevalence of purely monetary social relationships. In one of the classic community studies, *Middletown* by Robert and Helen Lynd, a leading citizen of the town explained to the authors the local custom of "placing" newcomers to Middletown by where they live, the size of their house, the kind of car they drive, and similar monetary externals: "It's perfectly natural," he said. "You see, they know money, and they don't know you." And of course the rational and anonymous social relations which one finds in so much of metropolitan New York made the Genovese case possible, if not inevitable or excusable. It should be pointed out, however, that since anonymity and mobility lie at the very roots of our kind of society, they must be understood rather than denounced, as has too often been characteristic of a great deal of social criticism, to say nothing of the denunciations of the thirty-eight Kew Gardens residents by the mass media at the time of the Genovese case.

An understanding of the need for anonymity in modern society has nowhere been discussed more wisely than in a recent book, *The Secular City*, by Harvey Cox. After carefully describing what social theorists like Professor Nisbet mean by *primary* (intimate, emotional, continuous, and communal) as against *secondary* (rational, impersonal, segmental, and functional) social relationships, Cox goes on, in a simple and matter-of-fact style, to illustrate the differences:

> Having lived both as a villager and as an urbanite I know just what these terms mean. During my boyhood, my parents never referred to "the milkman," "the insurance agent," "the junk collector." These people were, respectively, Paul Weaver, Joe Villanova, and Roxy Barazano. All of our family's market transactions took place within a web of wider and more inclusive friendship and kinship ties with the same people. They were never anonymous. In fact, the occasional salesman or repairman whom we did not know was always viewed with dark suspicion until we could make sure where he came from, who his parents were, and whether his family was "any good." Trips to the grocery store, gasoline station, or post office were invariably social visits, never merely functional contacts.

rural

There was little mobility or anonymity in the small Pennsylvania community in which Professor Cox grew up. Status-seeking and the compulsion to conform were unthought-of in a world where everyone had his place in an intricate web of primary relationships. Nor would anything quite like the Genovese case have been possible. On the other hand,

Professor Cox sees the inevitability of anonymity in our present urban environment. He writes:

> Now, as an urbanite, my transactions are of a very different sort. If I need to have the transmission on my car repaired, buy a television antenna, or cash a check, I find myself in functional relationships with mechanics, salesmen, and bank clerks whom I never see in any other capacity. These "contacts" are in no sense "mean, nasty or brutish," though they do tend to be short, at least not any longer than the time required to make the transactions and to exchange a brief pleasantry. Some of these human contacts occur with considerable frequency, so that I come to know the mannerisms and maybe even the names of some of the people. But the relationships are unifacted and "segmental." I meet these people in no other context. . . . The important point here is that my relationships with bank clerks and garagemen are no less human or authentic merely because we both prefer to keep them anonymous. . . . Urban anonymity need not be heartless. Village sociability can mask a murderous hostility.

All too many of us are more or less nostalgic about the good-old-days of spatial cohesion in the small, local community. But modern urban man must guard his privacy precisely because he needs to have many many more social relationships than in the past; consequently, he must of necessity keep most of them on the secondary level in order to reserve time for the few, more meaningful, primary relationships which we all need. Moreover, rather than being rooted in vicinage, kinship, and place, urban man's primary relationships are more likely to be based on free choice and common interests. Professor Cox illustrates this point by referring to a survey of attitudes among high-rise-apartment dwellers by some Protestant clergymen; they were horrified to find that many of the residents simply did not want to know their neighbors socially, but preferred to choose their friends elsewhere in the city. Inevitably, there is a certain amount of loneliness in any large city and perhaps especially among apartment dwellers. But is it not just these people who have firm friends on a transcommunal basis, gained along with professional, cultural, and recreational interests, who are the very ones who do not have time for extensive neighborhood sociability? What is needed is not condemnation but a realization that urban man has, as it were, come of age (all childhood social relationships, both now and in the past, have been based on kinship and propinquity), and is seeking new kinds of transcommunal friendships and voluntary associational loyalties.

For the student of history (which is essentially a record of the everchanging nature of social relationships), it is important to ask the right questions about the present, rather than to seek pat answers in some idealized past. For perhaps the problem of neighborliness is as old as recorded history. In this connection, it might be helpful to recall that the Judeo-Christian ethic grew out of the experiences of a mobile people who replaced the idolatries of place (Baal), which characterized the religions of more settled peoples, with the universal God (Yahweh) of history and eternal time. But in spite of the fact that now *all* men were supposed to be brothers under the fatherhood of *one* God, neighborly responsibility was still a problem, as the Good Samaritan parable in the New Testament suggests. Thus, the man who fell among thieves and was left half dead on the road from Jerusalem to Jericho was no more a next-door neighbor of the Samaritan than of the priest or the Levite, both of whom passed by on the other side of the road. Yet the Samaritan helped this stranger in an efficient and unsentimental way by bandaging his wounds, taking him to a nearby inn, and paying the innkeeper to look after him. In this parable, Jesus was not engaged in decrying the decline of community cohesion but in showing us what a moral man would do in an impersonal situation.

Rather than lament the loss of traditional community ties in the Kew Gardens of America, then, it would be wiser to try to understand what neighborliness means in a large-scale and urban society. First of all, modern man can never return to the communal mores of Main Street, with its attendant tyrannies of gossip and overheard conversations on the party line. His moral duty is no longer reinforced by the social sanctions of his next-door neighbors.

This means that urban society places far more emphasis on individual morality and personal ethics than is the case under simpler social structures. Is this too much to expect of men? Do we perhaps need laws to replace the older communal sanctions? Our Anglo-Saxon traditions, in contrast to those of continental Europe, for instance, do not legally require us to come to the aid of a person in danger. Yet the reader should ask himself whether or not he prefers our kind of voluntary society, which still emphasizes privacy and the minding of one's own business, to the more communal and cohesive, but perhaps more restrictive, societies of the Continent, where legal Samaritanism, or enforced neighborliness, is now found on the statute books of fifteen out of sixteen nations. The Russians have had such legal sanctions since 1917, for example, and the Germans ever since the Nazis instituted such laws in 1935. It is this kind of question—that is to say, how can old and perennial problems be handled in ways more suitable to new situations—which will be raised throughout this book. In the meantime, it might be well to outline briefly, by way of a few historical facts, how and why urban America came to be the way it is today.

II

By and large, it may be said that, until the Civil War, or perhaps through the 1870s, most Americans grew up and lived most of their lives in more or less small communities where social relationships were predominately of the communal type defined by Professor Nisbet and illustrated by Professor Cox's picture of his boyhood. Not only were the majority of social relationships within the various class levels close and diffuse rather than impersonal and segmental, but also, and perhaps of more importance, community leaders were usually bred locally and were accustomed to making decisions on the basis of first-hand knowledge of, and primary relations with, members of the other class levels, especially their constituents or employees.

Thus, Richard Hofstadter, in the following passage in his *Age of Reform,* shows how the "old gentry" once ruled America:

> Up to about 1870, the United States was a nation with a rather broad diffusion of wealth, status, and power, in which men of moderate means, especially in the many small communities, could command much deference and exert much influence. The small merchant or manufacturer, the distinguished lawyer, editor, or preacher, was a person of local eminence in an age when local eminence mattered a great deal.

All this is not to deny, of course, that local paternalism did not produce its share of cruelty and injustices as between social and economic classes.

In many ways, the decade of the 1880s marked a turning point in our history and the birth of the urban, centralized, and highly organized society which characterizes our twentieth-century world. At our first census in 1790, for instance, 95 percent of the American people were living on farms and engaged in agriculture; in the 1880s, for the first time, less than half the population was engaged in agriculture. At the same time, while no city in the United States had as many as 50,000 inhabitants in 1790, and only two exceeded 25,000, it was in the 1880s that our first city, New York, reached a million in population (today we have five cities with more than a million inhabitants and more than a hundred between 100,000 and a million in size). In fact, today we are virtually an urban nation, that is, some three-fifths of our population now reside in 168 metropolitan areas.

Urbanization was, of course, the product of industrialization and the resulting increase in the production of wealth. Between 1870 and 1900 the national wealth quadrupled, then doubled again by 1914. And this new wealth became increasingly centralized in the hands of a few. In 1891, *Forum* magazine published an article, "The Coming Billionaire," which estimated that there were 120 men in the nation worth over $10 million. The next year, *The New York Times* published a list of 4047 millionaires, and the U.S. Census Bureau estimated that 9 percent of the nation's families owned 71 percent of the wealth.

This new inequality of wealth was accompanied by an increasing centralization of business power. President Eliot of Harvard, in a speech before the Phi Beta Kappa society in 1888, noted this new corporate dominance when he pointed out that, while in that year the Pennsylvania Railroad had gross receipts of $115 million and employed more than 100,000 men, the Commonwealth of Massachusetts had gross receipts of only $17 million and employed no more than 6000 persons. And this corporate economy was further centralized financially on Wall Street. The capital required to launch the United States Steel Corporation, for example, would at that time have covered the costs of all functions of the federal government for almost two years. The centralization of entreprenurial and family capitalism in larger and larger corporate structures preceded, and indeed anticipated, the eventual growth of the state and the federal bureaucracy. J. P. Morgan and his associates, who put together the steel empire, were in almost unregulated control of a national corporate system.

These newly rich captains of industry and their families gradually formed a new, urban and national upper class, increasingly divorced from any local community roots or organic ties with the rest of society. As rootless and parvenu aristocrats, they engaged in all sorts of conspicuous consumption and irresponsible behavior which, in turn, was minutely chronicled in the national press. It was no wonder that the laboring classes lost faith in these new absentee-owners who now made decisions on Wall Street, decisions reflecting financial rather than human concern, and which affected the lives of thousands of anonymous workers and their families in countless mining and manufacturing towns throughout the nation. And some of the bloodiest civil disorders in our history, such as the Haymarket Square riot and the Homestead steel and Pullman strikes, were paralelled by passionate criticism of anonymous capitalism, which ranged from the writings of Edward Bellamy, Henry George, and Thorstein Veblen to the slogans and creeds of such protest movements as anarchism and socialism, the Populists, Grangers, Knights of Labor, and so forth. The irresponsible and crude behavior of the members of this new, national elite and the consequent mistrust which arose throughout the rest of society will be treated in more detail in the first two selections in this book. Here, it is enough to stress that it was the *search for community* which lay behind the various protest writings and movements in the Age of Reform, beginning in the late nineteenth century and continuing through the New Deal. The tone and style of the Marxian criticism of classical capitalism, for instance, are suggested in the following famous lines from the *Communist Manifesto:*

> The bourgeoisie, wherever it has got the upper hand, has put an end to all feudal, patriarchal, idylic relations. It has pitilessly torn asunder the motley feudal ties that bound man to his "natural superiors," and has left remaining no other nexus between man and man than naked self-interest, than callous "cash payment." It has drowned the most heavenly ecstacies of religious fervour, of chivalrous enthusiasm, of philistine sentimentalism, in the icy waters of egotistical calculation. It has resolved personal worth into exchange value. . . .

The Christian Socialists in England took seriously Marx's diagnosis of the ills of laissez-faire capitalism; at the same time, they sought different solutions to the problems of community disintegration, among them the founding of Toynbee Hall in London's East End in 1884. Thus began the settlement house movement, which almost immediately spread to America.

Members of the "old gentry" referred to by Hofstadter, and especially their college-educated sons and daughters, not only suffered from the status revolution which was pushing them out of power in the new corporate America; many of them, gradually realizing that the callous cash nexus was creating increasing affluence at the top of society, along with increasing poverty at the bottom, eventually became absorbed in the social gospel and settlement house movements, which, in turn, fed into the Progressive movement led by Theodore Roosevelt, Wilson's New Freedom, and Franklin D. Roosevelt's New Deal. One of the most inspiring leaders of the settlement house movement in this country was Jane Addams. Her father, a pious Quaker and successful business entrepreneur, had been one of the "old gentry" in a small town in Illinois. Upon completing college and receiving a legacy from her recently deceased father, Jane Addams traveled abroad in the 1880s. She was so horrified at the conditions in London's East End, and so impressed with the valuable work being done at Toynbee Hall, that she returned to America and, with Ellen G. Starr, founded Hull House in Chicago in 1889. In the meantime, settlement houses were being founded in most major cities along the Eastern Seaboard. In many ways, the settlement house movement was an attempt at institutionalizing a new kind of neighborliness, as the following passage from an early history of the movement suggests:

> A settlement is a colony of members of the upper classes, formed in a poor neighborhood, with the double purpose of getting to know local conditions of life from personal observation, and of helping where help is needed. The settler gives up the comfort of a West End home, and becomes a friend of the poor. He sacrifices to them his hours of leisure, and fills his imagination with pictures of misery and crime, instead of with the impressions of beauty and happiness. For a shorter or longer time the slum becomes his home. . . . The settler comes to the poor as man to man, in the conviction that it means a misfortune for all parties and a danger for the nation, if the different classes live in complete isolation of thought and environment. He comes to bridge the gulf between the classes. . . .

The ugliness, political corruption, and the various lower-class pathologies which social scientists and settlement house workers were trying to do something about, at the same time produced the flight to the suburbs which began first among the rich during the last part of the nineteenth century. Thus, the wealthy citizens of Boston, according to Justice Brandeis, told their sons: "Boston holds nothing for you except heavy taxes and political misrule. When you marry, pick out a suburb to build your house in, join the Country Club, and make your life center about your club, your home and your children." The Country Club, first of its kind in America, was founded in a Boston suburb in 1882. And suburban America remained largely an upper-class preserve until after World War I. During the prosperous twenties, the more affluent members of the middle classes moved in droves to new developments typified by "Floral Heights," built by George F. Babbitt, whose life and values were immortalized in Sinclair Lewis' novel, *Babbitt*. But the real flood began after World War II, when more and more members of the lower-middle class, and of the white working class as well, fled from what were becoming the urban Negro ghettos in the postwar suburban development boom symbolized by the Levittowns of Long Island, New Jersey, and Pennsylvania. The bulldozer, the moving van, and the traffic jam became major symbols of our postwar affluence; country clubs spread across the land and the new democratization of status seeking was now symbolized by millions of lost golf balls.

While, according to the 1960 census, two-thirds of the American people resided within 168 standard metropolitan areas, most of them were living in the white suburban fringe; the Negroes and other poor minority groups were crowded into the central cores of the great cities. Between 1950 and 1960, for instance, the population of the nation as a whole increased by 18 percent, that of the center, or "inner," cities by only 11 percent, and of the suburbs by over 50 percent. During this same period, New York City lost 1.5 percent of its population while the surrounding suburbs gained by 75 percent.

The suburban trend, of course, reflects a tremendous increase in social mobility. According to the U.S. Department of Commerce, one-half of the American people changed houses or apartments between 1955 and 1960; in Florida and California, the most rapidly growing states in the Union, 65 percent of the population moved during this period. The city of Los Angeles, sometimes referred to as "six suburbs in search of a city," is situated in one of the most mobile areas of the nation. While the Boston-to-Washington urban complex increased by some 15 percent between 1950 and 1960, for example, the San Francisco-to-San Diego complex increased by over 50 percent. One-tenth of the automobiles in the nation are now registered in California.

There is every indication that excessive social mobility and the resulting rootlessness breed insecurity and various forms of extremism. It is perhaps no accident that Henry Wallace, representing the extreme Left, did remarkably well in southern California in the Presidential campaign of 1948; similarly, Barry Goldwater, representing the extreme Right in the 1964 campaign, was very popular in southern California, but he lost some of the more cohesive suburbs in the East to the Democrats for the first time in the twentieth century. Also, various fringe sects, cults, and crusades, such as the John Birch Society and the Jehovah's Witnesses, which Professor Nisbet sees as substitute communities that arise when normal social relationships prove inadequate, have attracted a multitude of followers in and around the Los Angeles area.

Whereas at the turn of the century the nation's press and members of the intellectual community were largely concerned with the growing irresponsibility and selfishness of America's business and financial leaders and with the consequent unrest of the working class, during the past few years in America the mass media and concerned intellectuals have focused their attention on the unrest on the nation's campuses. Given the fact of the more general insecurity, mistrust, and alienation which seem to be characteristic of California's adult population today, it would seem quite natural that this national (and international) concern should have come to a head in the fall of 1964, when the Free Speech Movement (FSM) led a revolt on the Berkeley campus of the University of California.

The causes of today's unrest on the campuses of the nation are of course highly complex and vary from institution to institution. Much of it is due, however, to the decline in community as between the leadership and their student followers. Much like their business predecessors in the Gilded Age, members of the academic community have only recently achieved a position of relative affluence and prestige. And, quite like the businessmen and financiers whose decisions were based on their own financial self-interest rather than on the human needs of their employees, the more highly mobile members of the present academic community, especially at high (yet new)–prestige institutions, such as Berkeley, have lost human contact with the mass of anonymous students, both undergraduate and graduate. History sometimes seems to repeat itself in strange ways. In 1864, George Mortimer Pullman built his first sleeping car. In 1894, the inhabitants of his model company town, Pullman, Illinois, started a devastating strike because they had lost faith in their superiors, who had felt it necessary to cut back their wages. In 1964, many of the students on the idyllic Berkeley campus were moved by a similar feeling.

III

The nine essays which follow elaborate in more concrete detail the issues which we have tried to place historically and analytically in this introduction. These essays, it is hoped, will raise many questions in the reader's mind. All of them have to do with one central problem: How can a society institutionalize new social and legal relationships which will best promote a mature and responsible neighborliness appropriate to an urban, bureaucratized, and rational (rather than local and patriarchal) social order?

Perhaps it will be helpful to close this introductory essay with a few of the questions that will naturally arise. Was not the search for new types of communal relationships the central theme of the Age of Reform, from Progressivism through the New Deal? What was the relationship between the development of the graduated income tax and the glaring inadequacies of private charity and other voluntary forms of *noblesse oblige* in the complex and bureaucratized society which America had become in the course of the first part of the twentieth century? Was the passing of income tax legislation related to the conspicuous consumption and irresponsible behavior of the American plutocracy at the turn of the nineteenth century? How does legislation giving workers the right to organize and strike for better working conditions reflect the decline of local paternalism and the rise of anonymous and transcommunal capitalism? Does a strike function to create an *esprit de corps* among lonely laborers and give them an increased sense of being in control of their own destinies? How are minimum-wage laws, workmen's compensation insurance, and the guaranteed annual wage related to absentee ownership and the need for status, rather than purely contractual, relationships in a large corporate society? Are seniority laws in unions related to the decline in craft apprenticeship and the rise of a machine process within which a week's training can enable teen-age boys to do routine tasks with far more dexterity than their fathers who have had ten to twenty years of experience? How has the decline in apprenticeship affected the authority structure in the modern family, as well as in the plant and in society as a whole?

Are not executives reacting in much the same way as the workers in the plant to the large corporation structure? Why are modern executives often more interested in the quality of retirement plans and other welfare benefits than in salary structure alone? Why is a business executive today more likely to be known as Mr. Van Smith, vice-president of X Company, than as Mr. Van Smith of 123 High Street, in Xville? Why have United Fund contributions increased considerably in those communities where giving is now solicited at one's place of work rather than at one's home or by a neighborhood drive? Should corporations encourage and reward their executives for remaining in one community over a long period of time, or should promotions depend on their willingness to move every two or three years? How is the rise of professionalism in recent years—and the formal codes of ethics which it implies—related to the need for social control and community responsibility in an anonymous urban society?

How should urban redevelopment take into account the need for community? If architecture is a sociological and psychological as well as an aesthetic and engineering profession, is it not true that a high-rise apartment building on Park Avenue, where most of the occupants will have primary relationships based on their professional, cultural, and recreational interests, is quite different sociologically from a structurally similar apartment in the slums where, of necessity, primary relations are far more likely to be based solely on propinquity? Was the replacement since the war of some tens of thousands of elevator operators (potential Good Samaritans) in New York City by automatic controls based on the profit motive and the worship of electronic efficiency or on a real concern for human needs and safety?

How closely is the suburban movement related to a nostalgic desire for Main Street homogeneity and the mores of propinquity? Is the return to the suburban church and synagogue in postwar America based on a sincere seeking for religious expression, or is it a response to the need for community roots and status for oneself, and especially for one's children? At the same time, how is the modern church, particularly now that so much financial support is rooted in the suburbs, going to organize itself in such a way as to promote unity, rather than separation, between races and classes of men? How are traditional political boundaries to be reorganized in our large metropolitan areas so as to relate the talent in the suburbs with the social problems in the center cities?

All these questions and many more like them will occur to the readers of the selections which follow. Some will be disturbing, many requiring discouraging answers. Yet, just as the rhythms of nature demand that the budding rebirths of springtime be preceded by the dying fall and dormant winter, so the forces of rebirth and renewal in human society, so often unnoticed, or misunderstood and therefore feared and resisted, are always preceded, or paralleled, by apparently destructive social forces and the dying out of ancient traditions, so noticeable primarily because so vigorously defended. In this connection, it is well to recall that within a year of the Genovese case we Americans were witnessing one of the greatest outpourings of mass Samaritanism in our history. Thus, the Selma-Montgomery march, supported by many clergymen-heirs of the Social Gospel movement of the last century and understandably feared by many other sincere people, was a witness to our continuing concern for reform, and the never-ending quest for a more moral community in America.

The Separation of Rulers from the Community

SEBASTIAN DE GRAZIA

One of the main weaknesses of democracy, as social theorists from Aristotle to Tocqueville have pointed out, is that it so often leads to plutocracy, or the rule of the rich in their own rather than the people's interests. The loss of a sense of community and trust between leaders and the rest of the people is a problem which has faced most societies in history, especially in periods of rapidly increasing wealth and complexity of social organization. Few ruling classes have taken seriously Cato's repeated warnings to his fellow Roman senators who, as their wealth increased after the Punic Wars, gradually lost their traditional sense of duty and *gravitas*. The conspicuous consumption, increasing divorce rate, and all manner of self-indulgence that followed eventually led to the decline of Republican freedom and to the rise of autocratic Caesarism.

In the newly rich urban society which America became after the Civil War, similar behavior spread among the powerful industrialists who dominated the country in classic plutocratic style. The story of this "Gilded Age" has been told many times by historians, but never in a more compact and to-the-point manner than in the following selection.

THE EMINENT POLITICAL SCIENTIST, GAETANO MOSCA, ONCE MADE the following important generalization after noting certain similar phenomena among the feudal Poles, Irish, English, and Russians:

From Sebastian De Grazia, *The Political Community: A Study in Anomie,* University of Chicago Press, pp. 74–75, 115, 112. Reprinted without footnotes by permission of the author.

When the elementary needs of life are to an extent satisfied, what mostly contributes to creating and maintaining friction between rulers and subjects is not so much difference in possession of material goods as membership in two different environments. To take from Mosca's book, *The Ruling Class,* one example, the Polish nobles in the Middle Ages levied almost all the produce of their serfs, beat them, chose the most buxom of their daughters for their households, and otherwise "exploited" them. Yet the peasants never rebelled and "suffered the very bread to be snatched from their mouths that their lord might buy horses and costly weapons for hunting and for sabering Turks and Russians." All this, so long as he remained with them, spoke their language, swore the same oaths, ate the same kind of food, wore the same style of clothes, exhibited the same manners or lack of them, had same rustic superstitions. But from the time when he adopted the French ruffled dress and minced speech, gave luxurious balls after the manner of Versailles and tried to dance the minuet, "peasantry and nobility became two peoples apart." The serfs grew reluctant to support him, revolted periodically and viciously, despite the fact that part of their lord's newly acquired French education was a "more humane" treatment of his subjects—allowing them a greater share of the crops, namely, a higher standard of living, and less arbitrary treatment. This example illustrates a string of circumstances which convinced the members of the community (in this case, the serfs) that the lord to whom they paid homage no longer made their commonweal his primary concern. In other words, they felt that he had deserted them and that they could no longer rely on him to protect them from enemies, defend their faith, and represent them to God.

It may well be that an analogous event never occurred in the United States; still there is one period in American history which bears a striking resemblance and should be briefly discussed in this light even though the evidence falls short of proof.

It is almost a banality to repeat that in the United States the rise of the labor movement has not been colored by the presence of intense class consciousness or class hatred. But the last quarter of the nineteenth century was a time when this proposition did not hold. A series of labor explosions—1877, 1886 (there were eighteen hundred labor conflicts in this year alone), and 1894—shattered the peace of the period. Haymarket, Homestead, and Pullman are names of three of the bloodiest riots in America's chronicles. Public indignation heightened the blasts of trust-busters and muckrakers. Three now famous critics of capitalism levied their attack—Bellamy, Veblen, Henry George. Memberships swelled in radical organizations; new causes—Populists, Grangers, Socialists, Knights of Labor, Nationalist clubs, bands of the type led by

"General" Coxey—sprang up like weeds; armies of unarmed men from all parts of the country marched on Washington. If ever there was class consciousness, it descended on the United States in these years. Whereas before, mass movements of various kinds could have been called radical, these agitations were often revolutionary in the full sense of the word. Inflammatory utterances like that of Governor Waite of Colorado, "It is better that blood should flow to the horses' bridles," filled the air. Propertied persons shivered in apprehension of imminent rebellion. Terrified by strikes, riots, and bombings, they demanded the building of armories in cities. Backed by government cooperation, they crushed with a thoroughness born of fear every stir of radicalism, employing for the purpose police, militia, injunctions, and Pinkertons. On the other side, the muckrakers: Tarbell, Steffens, Baker, Samuel Hopkins Adams, Myer, Russell, Lindsey; the novelists: Howells, Norris, Sinclair, Garland; the scholars: Ross, Croly, Smith, and Lloyd; all testified to the sin and iniquity of the rich. How did this happen in a country so indisposed to class hatred?

The only serious theory given for the frenzied and violent hatred of this period is an economic one. The writers and the historians have more or less taken for granted that the vituperative upheaval naturally followed the sporadic declines in these years of the incomes of farmers and workers. But it is risky to assume that if a wage cut of, say, 10 per cent is announced by a firm, a strike or revolt will ensue. The thesis that class hatred and revolts are provoked by intolerable poverty or hardship in the lower strata of the population does not stand up under scrutiny. Revolutions have occurred in good times and bad with almost equal frequency, and, conversely, they have been absent in times both of severe economic contraction and of general well-being. Indeed if even semistarvation is widespread, rebellion becomes physically impossible. Will disappears with energy. If the flesh is weak, the spirit is unwilling.

One of the few quantitative studies in existence relating economic conditions to social disorders applies in part to this particular case. The economist A. H. Hansen analyzed the number of strikes and strikers in the United States and Canada for the period from 1881 to 1897, a decade and a half of falling prices. The coefficient of correlation between wholesale prices and the number of strikers was —0.388, in the author's own words, a "not entirely convincing relationship." Moreover, the most careful economic analysis of this period makes it difficult to say that the *real earnings* of the workers, agrarian and industrial, actually declined greatly. In fine, the unsupplemented economic theory falls short of real persuasiveness.

The necessary supplementary fact may be that the leaders of business, absorbed in the rich industrial aftermath of the Civil War, enthusiastically overstepped the bounds in their haste to adopt what they thought to be the appropriate way of life of an elite:

> The last two decades of the nineteenth century offered a spectacle of parvenudom without a peer. Ostentatious display was given the utmost press publicity, for a man like "Silver Dollar" Tabor was only too anxious to have the world know that even the door-knobs in his palace were of silver. No more abashed in their magnificence than royalty of the European baroque, were the American business men, who had, like kings, made a nation; but the splendor of kings had seemed, not personal, but an integral aspect of their office. . . . It was this difference which caused the naïve whims of the new-rich to exercise so fatal an effect on the public mind of America. . . . In Waldorf's "Peacock Alley" and in San Francisco's "Poodle Dog," millionaires paraded in their newest finery. . . . The very streets of the cities became filled with visions of elegance: ladies "like butterflies . . . with their brilliant and vari-colored dresses, their glittering jewels, their air of sprightly and reckless extravagance." Beside them stalked imposingly solid men: "glossy-headed old nabobs with rubicund noses, bald foreheads, heavy side whiskers, portly bodies and great watch seals, types of prosperous sons of commerce; there are dapper little dandies and ponderous big dandies."

Their wholesale adoption of supposed English customs and clothes, Renaissance paintings and sculpture, Roman orgies and extravaganzas, and extended sojourns on the Continent was well publicized in the press of the day. Nor was the public completely unaware that titled foreigners were being handed five hundred American daughters and two hundred and twenty million American dollars. In these crucial years the society page made its real debut.

Anyone living in the Gilded Age could have recounted numerous tales of the great, their rivalrous expenditure and waste galore. Now ordinarily in well-knit political communities people like to believe the *ruler* lives richly and gives generously—so long as he remains one of them, so long as he is *their ruler*. Even if they are themselves living on a bare subsistence level, they will see that he gets the lion's share. But in this period the captains of industry unwittingly separated themselves from the community at a time when they should have been reaffirming mutual ties. The introduction of Savile Row trouser cuffs was greeted on the streets with the taunt, "It must be raining in London." Some of the "swells" of the time tried what Mencken abbreviates as PSP—British public school pronunciation. Many individuals experimented with "been," "jolly well," "dontcherknow," "right you are," and "frightfully"; while at the same time "high tea became a fashionable rite, and pink coats came into favor among huntsmen." A song of the late eighties went to the heart of the matter:

> O, the things that we say and the queer things we do
> Are "English, you know! Quite English, you know!"

By importing alien cultivation, accents, clothes, and manners, they repudiated their leadership of a community which had believed in them and banked on their support. In a figurative sense they deserted their family in an hour of need. And in a literal sense, too, for the cult of the freshly discovered family tree dates from this period's race for genealogies, coats of arms, and sundry other proofs of European roots. Another event of the day which may have held a like meaning for the populace was the vast immigration from Europe. The "taking of jobs from Americans" and the giving of them to foreigners, although a logical result of the internationalism of capitalism, must surely have added to the feelings of neglect. In the political system of beliefs, preference should be shown the citizen. Even had the times been good, such action would have created great resentment and disunity. The mass embracing of third-party movements, of panaceas like the single tax, and of utopias like the Nationalist clubs (which, inspired by Edward Bellamy, numbered one hundred and sixty-three in the year 1891) indicated that people felt leaderless and protectionless, without a system of beliefs to guide them in their troubles. In a word—anomic. And hatred fanned by the seeming hypocrisy of their rulers fiercely burned:

> Wall Street owns the country. It is no longer a government of the people, by the people, and for the people, but a government of Wall Street, by Wall Street, and for Wall Street. . . . Our laws are the output of a system that clothes rascals in riches and honesty in rags. The parties lie to us, and the political speakers mislead us. . . . The people are at bay, and the bloodhounds of money who have dogged us thus far beware!

The turbulence generated in spots of real economic distress, a turbulence which otherwise might not have grown, swiftly spread out of its local origins. The immediate situation was exploited by propagandists who—and this is what makes the gulf between *ruler* and ruled the crucial factor—by propagandists who, without a plan, were co-operating with fellow-propagandists in other areas by attacking a common symbolic enemy—the "Capitalist," the bloated monopolist, with checkered suit, white vest, top hat, heavy in paunch and jowl, and bedecked with a miscellaneous array of diamonds. The era gave birth to the greatest period of cartooning in American history. If, as one student of the subject says, the cartoonist "starves in times of brotherly love," in the three decades after 1875 he grew fat. A flood of cartoons and caricatures arose mocking the *ton* and the aping of English customs. The century culminated in the Bradley Martin ball of 1897 at the Waldorf, costing a third of a million dollars, while the next century began with the James Hazen Hyde ball at Sherry's to the somewhat thinner tune of $200,000. Was it any wonder that the public uproar drove both hosts into European exile?

The activities of the parvenu in this period bear an amazing resemblance to the phenomena described by Mosca. In the Bradley Martin ball, for example, not one "restored feather on a pheasant served *à la mode*" escaped popular notice. Even the fact that for days a *quadrille d'honneur* had been rehearsing at Mrs. Astor's under the tutelage of Professor Karl Marwig was brought to public attention by a scare headline in the *Times*. As for the Hyde affair:

> A gilded youth, James Hazen Hyde, eight years after the Bradley-Martin Ball at the Waldorf, gave one more brilliant at Sherry's which was transformed into the Palace of Versailles. But where Mrs. Martin had chosen the period of Louis XIV, Hyde selected one with yet more unfortunate associations, and greeted his guests in the robes of the ill-fated Louis XVI. Promptly the people intimated that they knew history too, and were prepared to play their part, if drama was desired. Amid the general roar of rage, a sweeping investigation was started which uncovered startling frauds in the Equitable Life Insurance Company, a concern bequeathed to Hyde by his father. Hastily abdicating, the "last of the Capetians" fled to France. But the popular storm, gathering volume, swept on to the muckraking and trust-busting explosion that carried Theodore Roosevelt to triumph.

It might be wondered, since many of the participants in these prodigalities were not far removed from "the generation of shirt-sleeves," how they could be so far removed from the pulse of the public. Mrs. Bradley Martin's statements and actions, for example, disclosed a yawning chasm between the upper and lower strata: "One morning at breakfast during the winter of 1896–7 Mrs. Bradley Martin, reading of depressed conditions and the sufferings of the poor, suddenly decided to have a ball 'to give an impetus to trade.' As she pursued this ideal it grew grander and grander, until she ended by stimulating trade to the extent of $369,200." An explanation for the lack of simple foresight may be found in the growth of trusts and absentee ownership in this period, a period generally described as in transition from industrial to finance capitalism and one which more and more separated the owner from his workers, interposing a wall of paper. Somewhat later Theodore Roosevelt recognized the trend with the following words:

> The old familiar, intimate relations between employer and employee were passing. A few generations before, the boss had known every man in his shop; he had called his men Bill, Tom, Dick, John; he inquired after their wives and babies; he swapped jokes and stories and perhaps a bit of tobacco with them. In the small establishment there had been a friendly human relationship between employer and employee.
>
> There was no such relation between the great railway magnates, who controlled the anthracite industry, and the one hundred and fifty thousand men who worked in their mines, or the half million women and children who were dependent upon these miners for their daily bread. Very few of these mine workers had ever seen, for instance, the president of the Reading Railroad. . . . The workman saw . . . that the labor problem was not only an economic, but also a moral, a human problem.

In 1867 stock tickers were installed on Wall Street. The following year the exchange dealt in securities to the value of three billion dollars, marking a good beginning for high finance.

Perhaps it is to be wondered instead, then, that someone did have enough presence of mind to summon Pinkerton detectives, even though they marred the illusion of a hall in Versailles, for rumors were afloat that persons had been caught planting bombs under the Bradley Martin home and that others planned to hurl them through the Waldorf's windows.

In seeking causes for the end of the embryonic revolution in this part of American history, one must not neglect the clear fact of *force majeure* in the hands of the authorities. This lone fact, however, cannot account for the quick collapse of the struggle, for the subsequent legality of mass movements, for the "business unionism" and "class collaboration" in succeeding years. Nor does it help much to cite the progressive legislation of 1896 to 1912 which greatly benefited neither labor nor "little business." But one thing is certain. All sources agree that after the popular storms of the era the difference in appearance between the big businessman and the rest of the population dwindled:

> This tendency was more marked after the popular storms of the "trustbusting" era; then business men put away flashy waistcoats

and embroidered braces and, from the heights to the depths, from the tremendous hog-slaughterers to the simplest salmon-canners, went into quiet suits and quiet manners, with mildly twinkling eyes. They assured biographers that, though "public-spirited," they were averse to public posts, that their hobbies were far from eccentric and their characters, simple and genial, were not distinguished in any particular. At the same time, they surrendered the passion for horse-flesh which has ever been associated with the social climbing of business men into a "horsy" feudal aristocracy; some went so far in their renunciation that they took up cow-fancying instead, as did the banker, James Stillman, who explained: "The more you see of horses the faster you get, but the more you see of cows, the more refined you get."

In 1911 the brother of Bradley Martin published a book entitled *The Passing of the Idle Rich.* Many persons have cited this work for the tales it contains of the lives of the profuse rich, but few have realized that it marks the beginning of a new philosophy of rulership. From the 1880's on there had been Catos warning the dominant group in the Republic to mend its ways, but Martin's book entombed a dying "age of arrogance." The public demanded that the gods reflect its own image. "Idleness," proclaimed Martin, "is doomed as a vocation." The queen bees, like the drones, began to ask one another what each did for a living. Businessmen penned volumes protesting the intensity of their labors and the simplicity of their tastes. By 1910 the American Baroque was over. As Miriam Beard concluded in her *History of the Business Man,* "If fond of displaying themselves in the robes of Bourbons, it must be said that the American rich were not so blind. They swiftly wrapped tissue paper about their crowns and put away their royal robes in moth-balls. . . . The American at least knew when to take off his Louis-Quatorze ruffles and hide away his wig and sword." In more ways than one, this was the end of a century.

The Factory in the Community

W. LLOYD WARNER AND J. O. LOW

The Yankee City Series, the study of a small and ancient New England community, is recognized as a major classic in sociology. It consists of five volumes published between 1941 and 1959. The research work, begun in 1930, was led by W. Lloyd Warner, who was assisted by a series of graduate students in social anthropology at Harvard University; most of the analysis was done by Warner and his graduate students at The University of Chicago. This selection, eventually included in volume IV (1947) of the series, attempts to show how a relatively stable period of local and patriarchal control of the shoe industry in Yankee City was gradually replaced by absentee ownership, centered in Boston and New York; how this change in social relations affected both management and worker; how craft status was replaced by task anonymity; and, above all, how a strike was an attempt on the part of the workers to gain a new and different sense of status through unionization. It brings a historical and analytical approach to bear on the problem of community in modern society.

THE AMERICAN SOCIAL SYSTEM HAS BEEN DRASTICALLY CHANGED by the development of our industrial institutions; on the other hand, our industrial organization has become what it is by virtue of being a part of the larger American social system. The two are interdependent and mutually influence each other, yet we know almost nothing about the nature of the relations that exist between the two. Much is known about the factory as a production and economic unit, but little is known about the influence of the factory on the community and the community on the factory. We shall attack the problem in the present

From *Industry and Society,* edited by William Foote Whyte. Copyright 1946. McGraw-Hill Book Company. Used without footnotes by permission.

chapter. To do so we shall concentrate our attention on one city where the factory and social system of the community were carefully studied over a period of years by a group of social anthropologists.

The relations of this factory and the community were studied when they were in equilibrium and the various parts of the factory and the city were well integrated and formed a functioning unit. They were also examined when industrial strife and social conflict had disrupted this equilibrium. Social anthropologists study periods of social disruption to gain deeper insight into what normally takes place in a social system because crisis periods reveal and dramatize the important and significant factors that often lie hidden during times of peace and quiet.

We are going to examine a strike in the shoe industry of an American community to learn what we can about the place of the factory in contemporary American life.

In the worst year of the depression all the workers in all the factories of the principal industry of a New England community walked out. They struck at management with little or no warning; they struck with such impact that all the factories closed and no worker remained at his bench. Management had said they would never strike, for the workers of Yankee City were sensible, dependable, and, by a long peaceful history, had proved that they would always stay on the job. Union men outside the city agreed that Yankee City could not be organized and held that the local shoe workers were obstinate and "always stupid enough to play management's game." Many of the workers had told us that there would be no strike. Most of the townspeople, from the autocrats of Hill Street to the people on city welfare in the clam flats, said Yankee City workers would never strike. But they did—the foreigners and the Yankees of 10 generations—the men and the women, the very old and the very young, Jews and Gentiles, Catholics and Protestants, the whole heterogeneous mass of workers left their benches and in a few hours wiped out most of the basic productive system from which Yankee City earned its living. Not only did they strike and soundly defeat management, but they organized themselves, joined an industrial union, and became strong union members.

The industrial battle was fought between the owners of seven factories and 1,500 workers. Four of the factories, "the larger ones," employed the vast majority of the workers and accounted for most of the "34,000-dollar weekly payroll." This industrial war lasted a month. It began on a bleak and snowy day in early March and lasted well into April. There were three clearly marked periods, each with different objectives and strategy and in each the industrial workers and the managers were dominated by different feelings.

In the first period, when management and the union fought desperately to gain control over the workers, the union was successful in organizing the workers and management was prevented from regaining control over them. The second period began when all the workers requested the union to represent them in the struggle with management and the union, secure with the workers organized behind them, began frontal attacks on management. During this time each continued its intense efforts to influence and dominate public opinion in Yankee City. The union also won this fight since the public identified the union with the workers and most of Yankee City sided with the shoe operators. The final phase, that of mediation and peace negotiations, began when a government labor board entered and started a series of negotiations that terminated the strike. Other efforts had been made from the beginning but none was successful.

The ultimate objective of each side, to which each fashioned its strategy was, of course, to make the other side capitulate and accept its demands; for management this meant the workers would return to their benches under approximately the same working conditions and wages as they had left; for the workers it meant that the management would agree to their demands and increase wages and improve working conditions; and for the union officials it meant that the union would maintain its control over the workers and keep them members of their organization, and management would be forced to deal directly with the union and not with the unorganized workers.

Each side organized itself and developed its strategies of offense and defense. The workers' defense tactics were centered around maintaining their unity and defeating management's offensive strategy of breaking up the workers' group and of destroying their morale. Accordingly, the workers used ritual and ceremonial procedures, where recognized symbols of solidarity, such as the flag, patriotic hymns, and the American Legion band played prominent parts. They achieved a defensive organization by means of meetings, speeches, entertainments, and the formation of a large number of committees that gave the mass of the workers opportunities to participate and to become and feel a part of a powerful and aggressive group. They took offensive action against management by making a series of demands for better wages and working conditions, by picketing, by making attacks against management in the newspaper, and by using the platform to influence public opinion. Management's defense was always to take the offense. The tactics tried included sending foremen to talk to the workers individually and thereby separating them from the group, spreading discouraging rumors, advertising in the paper, insisting on secret balloting by the workers when they voted on the issue of returning to work, and, above all, threatening to move their factories elsewhere should the workers continue with their demands and join the union. Of course, it must be remembered that each side, throughout the strike, was being deprived of its income, labor of its wages and management of its profits.

The strike occurred almost to the very year of the three hundredth anniversary of the founding of Yankee City and the beginning of the shoe industry. Shoemaking was always important there, but it was not until near the end of the nineteenth century that it achieved its place of supreme importance in the economy of the town. From the beginning, shipping, shipbuilding, fishing, and the other trades of the sea had dominated Yankee City's economic existence and set their mark on the community. When the New England shipping industries disappeared, Yankee City turned from the sea and sent its many drummers, salesmen, and manufactured goods westward to make the profits necessary for the establishment and continuance of its factory system. It was then that the textile manufacturers moved into the lead, but throughout the whole period shoemaking contributed significantly to the economic life of the city and, by the end of the century, had risen to a commanding place. Yankee City's shoe workers and owners throughout this time were known everywhere in the country for the excellence of their products.

Although the economy of the city went through revolutionary changes, the social superstructure that guided and maintained the lives of its citizens remained very much what it had been at the end of the War of 1812. The physical city stretches in a thin rectangle two miles inland along the bank of a large river from the harbor. Here, when the field study was made, lived 17,000 people. They were distributed from the river bottoms and clam flats back to the high ground on which Hill Street is located. The people of high status, some of them the descendants of those who made their fortunes in the sea trade, lived on this broad, elm-lined avenue. The people of lowest status, many of whom could trace their ancestry through long lines of fishermen to the city's founding, lived in Riverbrook on the clam flats. Between the two were the "Side-streeters" who, appropriately enough, occupied a middle-class status.

The upper class of Hill Street was composed of two levels; the "Old Families" who could trace their aristocratic position through an ancestry of many generations, and the "New Families" who had but recently achieved high status. In the latter group were several families who "got their money out of shoes." The upper middle and lower middle classes were very much like such people wherever they are found in the United States or, for that matter, in all English-speaking countries. They were the conservatives, who, dominated by a "Protestant ethic," maintained, and often controlled, the moral order of the city. Below them was the upper lower class composed of the "poor but honest workmen" who ran the factories. At the bottom were the "broken-down Yankees," often called the "Riverbrookers," who also worked in the factories and who did a moderate amount of clamming and fishing for a living.

Scattered throughout the status system from the lower upper class ("New Family" level) to the lower lower class ("Riverbrookers") were the descendants of the Irish and, at somewhat lower levels, the French-Canadians, Jews, Poles, Greeks, and other ethnic groups, who began settling in Yankee City in the 1840's and continued until 1924. They had their own social system that preserved an increasingly small stock of the ancestral culture while relating their populations to the larger world of Yankee City. The Yankees were dominant and the most powerful group in the city, but the ethnics each year increased their power and prestige while they shed their variant mores and accepted those of the dominant Yankees.

All these people were involved in the strike; the bread of most of them was directly or indirectly earned in the shoe factories. Men everywhere in the city asked themselves, when the strike occurred, why such a thing should have happened to the people of Yankee City. Each man had his own answer. The answer of each tended to reveal more about the life and status of the man who talked than about the cause or causes of the strike. More often than not the explanations were economic. These townspeople forgot that there had been serious depressions before and that there had been no strikes. Each of them forgot that there had been low wages before and that there had been no unions. Each forgot, too, that there had been strikes when wages were high and times were said to be good. Although these economic arguments supplied important and necessary reasons for the strike and the unionization of the workers, they were insufficient explanations.

It seems to us the secrets of industrial strife in Yankee City and elsewhere lie beyond the words and deeds of the strike. They can only be found in the whole life of the community in which the workers and owners are but a part. The answers of the economic determinists or of the historians, while important, are not sufficient.

If social science is to be of any worth to us, it must be capable of adding significance and meaning to human behavior that will give us deeper insight into human life and explain more fully than common-sense knowledge why human beings act the way they do. Science necessarily solves problems. To solve them it must know what questions need to be answered. Let us reexamine the questions implied in the statements of the Yankee City townsmen in a more explicit and pointed manner to determine if we can learn what happened in this industrial crisis and to see if such knowledge about the strike can tell us about other similar crises in American life.

The immediate questions are basic to the whole problem, but, of even greater importance, they lead us into more fundamental ones about the nature of our industrial society. We will endeavor to give at least partial answers to some of these larger questions.

The first questions we must answer about the strike are

1. In a community where there had been very few strikes and *no* successful ones, why did the workers in *all* the factories of the largest industry of the community strike, win all their demands and, after a severe struggle, soundly defeat management?

2. In a community where unions had previously tried and failed to gain even a foothold and where there had never been a union, why was a union successful in separating the workers from management?

3. Why was the union successful in organizing *all* the workers in *all* the shoe factories in the community?

4. Why was the union successful in maintaining the organization despite the intense and prolonged efforts of management to prevent unionization and break up the shoe union?

5. Why did Yankee City change from a nonunion to a union town?

Perhaps the best way to gain an understanding of the strike and of the relations of the contemporary factory and the community is to view the present in the light of the past. The history of Yankee City's shoe factories may be conveniently divided into four periods ranging from the earliest times when the family was the productive unit through the periods of early and late small-city capitalism to the present stage when mass production and the machine dominate the industry, and control has shifted to New York. Included were revolutionary technological developments, increases in the division of labor, radical modifications of ownership and control, and rearrangements of the relations of producer and consumer and of workers among themselves.

During the technological development of Yankee City's shoe industry, the tools changed from a few basic ones, entirely hand-used, to machines in an assembly line; and their product changed from a single pair of shoes to tens of thousands in mass production. In the beginning, the family made its own shoes or a highly skilled artisan, the cobbler, made shoes for the family. In time, several families divided the highly skilled jobs among themselves and their families. Ultimately, a central factory developed and the jobs were divided into a large number of systematized low-skilled jobs. The history of ownership and control is correlated with the changes in the division of labor. In early days, tools, skills, and materials were possessed by the family. Eventually the materials were supplied by the owner manager and soon he also owned the tools and machines. The sequence of development of producer-consumer relations tells a similar pointed story. The family produced and consumed its shoes all within the circle of its simple unit. Then, the local community was the consumer-producer unit, and ultimately the market became national and even world-wide. Workers' relations changed from those of kinship and family ties to those of occupation, where apprenticeships and craftsmanship relations were superseded, and the industrial union became dominant in organizing the affairs of the workers. The structure of economic relations changed from the immediate family into a local hierarchy, and the locally owned factory changed into a vast, complex system owned, managed, and dominated by New York City.

With these several histories in mind, let us ask ourselves what would have happened if the strike had taken place in each of the several periods. In period one, with a family consuming and producing economy, such a conflict would have been impossible. The social system had not evolved to sufficient complexity; the forces had not been born that were to oppose each other in civil strife. In the second phase, several families in a neighborhood might have quarreled but it is only in one's imagination that one could conceive of civil strife among the shoemakers.

In the third phase, however, there appears a new social personality, and an older one begins to take on a new form and assume a new place in the community. The capitalist is born and during the following periods he develops into full maturity. Meanwhile the worker loses control and management of his time and skills and becomes a subordinate in a hierarchy. There are, thus, distinct and opposing forces set up in the shoemaking system. What is good for one is not necessarily good for the other, but the interdependence of the two opposing groups is still very intimate, powerful, and highly necessary. The tools, the skills, and the places of manufacture belong to the worker, but the materials, the place of assembly, and the market are now possessed by the manager. Striking is possible but extremely difficult and unlikely.

In the fourth period, full capitalism has been achieved; the manufacturer is now the owner of the tools, the machines, and the industrial plant; he controls the market. The workers have become sufficiently self-conscious and antagonistic to machines to organize into craft unions. Industrial warfare still might prove difficult to start, although it did occur, because in a small city where most people know each other, the owner and manager more often than not knows "his help" and they know him. The close relation between the two often implies greater compatibility and understanding that cut down the likelihood of conflict. But when strikes do occur, the resulting civil strife is likely to be bitter because it is in the confines of the community.

In the last period, the capitalist has become the supercapitalist and the workers have forgotten their pride in their separate jobs, have dimissed the small differences among them, and have united in one industrial union with tens and hundreds of thousands of workers throughout the country combining their strength to assert their interests against management. In such a social setting strikes are inevitable and certain.

An examination of the status of the worker in the factory and in the community reveals another important factor contributing to industrial strife. During the early periods of the factory in Yankee City a skill hierarchy dominated the lives of the workers and helped establish their place in the community. The introduction of the machine into all parts of the production processes of the factory largely destroyed the skill hierarchy.

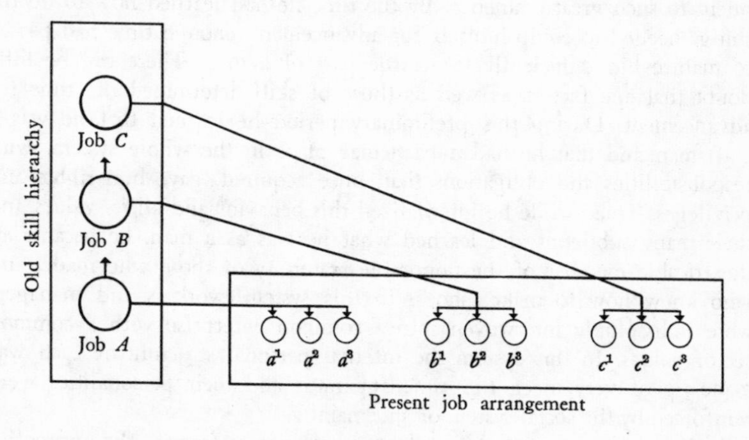

CHART I

Chart I illustrates what has happened to craft and skill in the modern factory. The vertical hierarchy of skilled jobs has become a horizontal layer of low-skilled ones. Each of the skilled jobs has been divided into a number of simple, low-skilled ones and machines are performing most of the actions necessary for each job. Jobs formerly at the top and bottom of the hierarchy that were separated by higher and lower prestige and paid accordingly are now in the same category of prestige and pay. We believe that the breakup of the skill hierarchy contributed importantly to the outbreak of the strike, to the course it took, and, in particular, to the coming of the union. The hierarchy of crafts that once organized the relations of the workers and provided a way of life for the shoe workers was really an age-grade system. Youngsters served their hard apprenticeship and, as neophytes, learned their task and, even more importantly, were taught to respect the skills they had learned and those they looked forward to learning. Above all, they acquired respect and admiration for the older men above them who had acquired the skills and who occupied the proud positions of journeymen and master craftsmen. These youngsters aspired to achieve for themselves a similar high position and to be the objects of a similar respect of their fellow craftsmen and fellow townsmen. Each young man, in direct face-to-face interaction with those above, imitated and learned a way of life while being highly motivated by the strong desire to escape the irksome limitations of his present low position and to attain the higher place where he would have the satisfaction of making his own decisions and possess the prestige and pay consequent to such great eminence. By the time he had learned how to do the things needed to equip himself for advancement, enough time had passed to mature him sufficiently to act the part of a man. There can be little doubt that age factors as well as those of skill determined the time for advancement. During this preliminary period he learned that he was a craftsman and that he had a particular place in the whole system, with responsibilities and obligations that, once acquired, gave him rights and privileges. Thus, while he internalized this behavior and all its values and their many subtleties and learned what he was as a man, he became an inextricable member of the honorable fraternity of those who made, and who knew how to make, shoes. In this system, workers and managers were indissolubly interwoven into a common enterprise with a common set of values. In this system the internal personal structure of each was made up of very much the same apparatus and their personalities were reinforced by the social system of shoemaking.

In learning to respect the skill of the master craftsman, the apprentice learned to respect himself. He had security in his job, but he had even greater personal security because he had learned how to respect it. And because he was a member of an age-graded male fraternity made up of other men like himself who had the knowledge and necessary skills to make shoes, he possessed that feeling of freedom and independence and of being autonomous that comes from leading a disciplined life. He spent his life acquiring virtue, prestige, and respect, learning as he aged and climbed upward and at the same time teaching those who were younger than he and who aspired to be like him.

Slowly this way of life degenerated and the machine took the virtue and respect from the workers, and at the same time broke the skill hierarchy that dominated their occupation. There was no longer a period for young men to learn to respect those in the age grade above them and in so doing to become self-respecting workers. The "ladder to the stars" was gone and with it much of the fabric of the "American dream."

When the age-grade structure that organized the male aborigines of Melanesia and North America into a hierarchy of prestige and achievement was broken under the impact of white civilization in many of these societies, the frustrations suffered by those who had once known self-respect crystallized into aggressive movements or into attempts to abolish the new ways and to retreat into the old and cherished ways of the past. There are, thus, some resemblances to developments in non-European societies.

The parallel between Yankee City's age-grade structure and theirs cannot be pushed too far but certainly the two share obvious characteristics. In the earlier days of the machine, the Knights of St. Crispin organized themselves and attempted to stop the further introduction of machinery, and most of them longed for the good old days when there were no machines, when a trained hand and eye did the job. These attempts failed and their organization collapsed, for they were not adaptive and could not stop the inevitable advance of our industrial technology.

When the whole age-grade structure of craftsmanship had almost entirely collapsed and the American shoe worker was thereby denied his share of the American dream, he and his kind were ready for any mass movement that would strike at those whom they charged, in their own minds, with responsibility for their unhappy condition. Much of this behavior was not conscious. Much of it was feeling rather than thought, as indeed were the feelings and thoughts that composed the mass movements of the aboriginal Melanesians and North American Indians. It seems certain, however, that American workers, taught from childhood that those who work and apply themselves and practice the ethics of the middle class would be rewarded by achievement and success, would rebel and strike back out of sheer frustration when they found out that the American dream no longer was true and that the hard facts belied the beautiful words they had been taught. It seems even more likely that the effects of the break in the skill hierarchy were potent forces that contributed their full share to the workers' striking and accepting the union as their champion.

Two other important causes of the strike must now be dealt with. The first is the expansion of the hierarchy upward, out of Yankee City, through the expansion of individual enterprises and the establishment by them of central offices in distant large cities. The second is the expansion of the structure outward from Yankee City through the growth of manufacturers' associations and labor unions, also with headquarters outside Yankee City and with units in many other shoemaking communities in New England and elsewhere. Both of these developments have gone on concurrently, each reacting upon the other. And both decrease Yankee City's control over its shoe factories by subjecting the factories, or segments of them, to more and more control exerted from outside Yankee City.

In the early days of the shoe industry, the owners and managerial staffs of the factories, as well as the operatives, were residents of Yankee City; there was no extension of the factory social structures outside the local community. The factories were then entirely under the control of the community; not only the formal control of city ordinances and laws, but also the more pervasive informal controls of community traditions and attitudes. There were feelings of neighborliness and friendship between manager and worker and of mutual responsibilities to each other and to the community that went beyond the formal employer-employee agreement.

In the days of local capitalism, the shoe manufacturers were accepted by all social strata as leaders of the total community. Shortly after the death of the most powerful of these business leaders, a number of prominent Yankee City men published a memorial volume that contained the usual words of high praise for great men. Since these same words, unlike those of many memorial volumes, were said about him by ordinary men of the street and were used during the strike, it is important to examine them. A member of one of the oldest families of Yankee City wrote:

> He [the manufacturer] was one of the most remarkable men ever connected with Yankee City; a businessman of liberal culture, of fine literary taste, gifted as an orator, in music and theatricals. . . . He was an acquisition to any society. He honored any public station, however high. . . . He achieved more in his fifty years of life than most men can point to after marking a very old age. . . .
>
> He was identified with the public health of this city and was a conspicuous figure in all its great social functions as long as his health permitted it. He was a leading financier and a man who at once took and ever afterwards occupied a prominent position in this community. For years, by common consent, he was the leading man of the city. . . . Forcefulness of character made him the commanding spirit in every undertaking in which he shared and in every circle in which he moved.

Our analysis of the manufacturer's participation in the community provides the crucial evidence to show why he became the powerful collective symbol that was used against the contemporary managers during the strike.

In the business and financial sphere he was

1. Owner and head of his million-dollar shoe company.
2. President of one of the most powerful banks in the city.
3. Member of the Board of Trustees of the Financial Institute, a firm of the utmost prestige and power in the community.
4. Director of the Security Trust Company, another powerful financial institution.
5. Director of the Yankee City Gas and Electric Company.

   He was involved in a large number of civic enterprises and was a member of many civic institutions. He was

6. Director and one of the founders of the city's most important hospital.
7. Director of the Public Library.
8. Member of the school committee.
9. Trustee of the Revere Free School.
10. President of the City Improvement Society.

    He also took an important part in politics. He was

11. Chairman of the Republican City Committee.
12. Member of the City Council.
13. Delegate to the National Republican Convention.
14. Mayor of the city.

    He was also prominent in church and religious affairs. He was

15. President of the Yankee County Unitarian Club.
16. President of the Yankee County Unitarian Conference.

    He was a leader in fraternal affairs and was

17. Past Master of St. John's Lodge.
18. Member of several important fraternal orders.

    He was an active member of some of the most exclusive clubs of the city, including

19. The Drama Club.
20. The Thursday Night Club.
21. The Friday Evening Club.
22. The February Club.
23. The Revere Club.
24. The Country Club.

The evidence demonstrates that in all these organizations he was active and powerful. This brief survey of some of his participation in the community demonstrates that his activities ramified throughout the city and that much of the life of the city was centered in him. It also demonstrates that he accepted responsibility for the larger affairs of the community and helped integrate its activities, for he provided responsible leadership for the whole life of the community. "He was a man you could depend on."

Very much the same could be said about his two successors. They, too, were responsible elders of the city. They not only provided jobs and wages through their factories, but they were citizens of the town and men who felt obligated to it. Their membership in local institutions compares very favorably with that of their predecessor.

In the days before big-city capitalism took control, the local enterpriser was financed by Yankee City banks. These banks and other investment houses possessed more autonomy and prestige then than they do now. In the development of the local shoe industry, local financiers played important and necessary roles and, at least part of the time, were silent partners in the business. Much of the wealth they derived from their investments was reinvested in Yankee City. The money was put into new enterprises, their own living, or civic activities. Their white Georgian houses on Hill Street, whose gardens bordered those of the manufacturers, were majestic symbols of their power and prestige and forever reminded and often reassured everyone of the visible presence of these powerful and protecting men in Yankee City.

The Yankee City financiers, too, were men of responsibility, dominated by sentiments of local pride. They did well for themselves, but they also did well for the city. Perhaps the price was high, but the product bought by the rest of the community was substantial and of high quality. Their philanthropies, combined with their power and leadership, contributed enormously to the city's development and provided a firm foundation for the larger civic life of the community. Parks, libraries, hospitals, societies to help the unfortunate and aged, foundations to send young men to college, endowments of schools, churches, and many other worthy civic enterprises were granted and maintained by the money and leadership of the local financiers and manager owners.

The essential point to remember for these leaders of industry and finance is that they were subject to local control (1) because they were dominated by local sentiments which motivated them "to take care of their own people," and (2) they were under the powerful influence of the numerous organizations to which they belonged and of their personal contacts with local citizens, which directly related them to influence from every part of the city.

The advent of big-city capitalism shattered this closely woven network of personal relations, loyalties, and obligations. Yankee City shoe factories are no longer owned exclusively by local citizens. More and more of them have been absorbed by larger enterprises whose executive offices are in New York City. At the time of our study, the largest shoe factory in Yankee City was owned by a company which operated several other factories in New England and which also owned the nationwide ABC chain of retail shoe stores, all of which were controlled from a central office in New York. Even some of the smaller Yankee City shoe factories, although still locally owned and managed, sold most of their shoes to chain-store organizations.

Yankee City has become but a pinpoint upon the map of industrial empire for these large investment houses. The flow of wealth from Yankee City's banks and factories, once a great local arterial system giving life and strength to the town, now has shrunk to an infinitesimal part of big-city, world-wide capitalism and is of no vital significance in the life of this great system.

The extent of this change may be seen from the following account of the finances of the ABC company, which appeared in a June, 1945, issue of a large New York newspaper:

> A group headed by Oppenheimer and Co. and Brandeis and Son, and including the Stultz Co., has concluded an agreement for purchase of the majority of Lion Shoe Corp. stock, it was announced today.
>
> Lion Shoe will be merged into its wholly owned retail subsidiary, the ABC Shoe Corp., with subsequent public issue of securities of the latter company.
>
> Abraham Cohen, associated with the companies in an executive capacity for more than 20 years, will be elected president and general manager. Frederick Stultz, president of the Stultz Co., will be made chairman of the board.
>
> The ABC Shoe Corp. owns a number of factories equipped to manufacture 20,000 pairs of shoes daily and operates a chain of 110 stores in 56 cities.

Decisions on these high levels of national and international finance are being made without regard for the needs and vital interests of Yankee City. The old ties between top management and the community have completely broken down.

As the vertical hierarchy of the factory system extended to executive offices in New York, even the local factory managers came to be, for the most part, "outsiders" and members of ethnic minorities. They had their factories in the town and some of them drove down to work in the morning and left at night. The workers knew or felt that the forces that controlled local men would not control these outsiders. The vast network of relations and memberships that made the former owners local leaders, as well as local manufacturers, had been reduced to a purely economic one of employer and employee. It was that and nothing more. It is small wonder that the workers during this strike "gave the horse laugh to the managers when they talked about being good fellows."

At the time of the strike the few local men who were managers, although born and reared in Yankee City, were little more than the factory managers for big-city capitalists, for they occupied inferior positions in this vastly extended vertical structure. They were not in a position to take leadership. They were not in a position of great power where they were free to make the decisions that always characterized the lives of the owners of the previous period.

Each of these local men felt what had happened very deeply and some of them were explicit enough about it to say so. We knew some of them well. They were not the weak or unscrupulous men that their opponents made them out to be. Personally, they were men of good reputations in the business world. Some of them had been trained by their own fathers to be community leaders but their place in the new socioeconomic structure of Yankee City prevented them from playing this role and each in his own way contributed directly to the defeat of the managerial group. Part of their ineptness was due to their inability to measure up in their own minds to the great men of the past. This was a dead past, glorious and safe, when men knew themselves to be free men and Yankee City was "the hub of the universe." This whole period was symbolized in the memories of the workers and management by the names and reputations of the former owners. The lives of these men epitomized the period for all those who remembered. They symbolized the longing of everyone to return to those days when it was possible for one of them, with all his power and prestige, to stop and gently chide Sam Taylor, the cutter, for not calling him by his first name, and he and Sam could talk about "the trouble in the cutting room." Power was under control and security was present then; manager and worker were part of a self-contained system in which each knew his part in the total system.

In these days of big-city capitalism, when Yankee City had lost control of its own destinies, few workers would go up to the "big boss" to tell him "what's wrong in the cutting room," and those who did were not considered the respected friends of the workers but "stool pigeons who were getting theirs from management."

During the strike the local men cut poor figures as fighters for management's side. Two of them openly lined up with the strikers. Local sentiment and the feeling against "the foreigners" was too much for them. They materially contributed to the workers' victory.

One of them damaged the cause of management when he tried to fight the head of the union during a peace conference. Everyone said he blustered and acted badly when he used such tactics! He was under the control of higher management and occupied an inferior managerial position where he had little freedom to assume command and take leadership. Yet he had learned from "one of the grand old men" of the last period, when he worked for him, how his kind of man should act and he knew that an owner and manager should assume control. It seems a reasonable hypothesis that the conflict between his beliefs on how a manager should act and what he was permitted to do by his status greatly contributed to causing his unfortunate act, an act which materially aided the union. He tried to take command in a situation where it was impossible to do so, and instead of commanding he could only "bluster."

His antagonist, on the other hand, was "top manager" of the union. He did have power and he could make decisions. His beliefs about what should be done and his status were commensurate and he used them to the greatest effect for the cause of the union.

All these local men knew somehow they were not the men their "fathers" were and these dead men, symbolizing the glorious past, overawed and helped defeat them. While the men of yesterday are dead, "their souls go marching on" in the memories of the living. They have become collective symbols of that lost age when the prestige and power of local financiers and local producers "took care of our own people." These symbols were powerful influences upon the sentiments of workers as well as managers during the strike crisis. Sapping the confidence of the local managers, they gave strength to the strikers who dramatized their cause in terms of a struggle of Yankee City against big-city capitalism.

From this analysis of today's and yesterday's owners several important propositions can be offered that contribute to our understanding of the strike. The vertical extension of the corporate structure of the shoe manufacturing enterprises had pushed the top of the hierarchy into the great metropolises and, in so doing, had brought in outsiders who were foreigners in culture, had no local prestige, and were lacking in understanding and feeling for the local workers and the town itself. This extension of the industrial hierarchy reduced the local men to inferior positions in the hierarchy, where they were incapable of making decisions and could not initiate actions that would give them the power of leadership for the workers and for the rest of the town.

The local managers, reduced to inferior statuses in the industrial hierarchy also occupied lower social class ranking in the community than their predecessors. This greatly reduced their strength as leaders who could form community opinion in times of crisis when the position of management was threatened. They could no longer lead the worker or the community. Because of this inferior position of the managers, those men in the community who would once have been their natural allies and who enjoyed top social class position were now above them and shared none of their interests, were hostile to them and friendly to the workers.

In "the good old days," the people of Yankee City felt that they all shared in a common way of life, in which business and industry was closely integrated into the community. This way of life had its frictions and conflicts, but it provided all the people with a set of common symbols to guide their behavior, and it also provided effective leadership from the top of the social order. Furthermore, these personal ties made it possible for workers to redress their grievances through going right up to members of management.

When New York financiers assumed control of the industrial hierarchy, the social and civic leaders of Yankee City were no longer active in local management. The management of industry was no longer directly tied in with the wider life of the community. This split between management and the community made it possible to mobilize the workers into an organization to fight management.

In the same period, the solidarity of the workers was strengthened by the breakup of the old skill hierarchy. No longer could the workers start at the bottom as apprentices and progress upward step by step as they grew older and acquired the skills and learned the way of life of the skilled craftsman. This age-graded skill hierarchy served to differentiate the workers from one another and to provide increasing security, prestige, and freedom with every step up from the bottom of the ladder. Now the rewards and satisfactions of this way of life are gone forever. Mechanization of the shoe industry has leveled the skills so that there is little room for such differentiation. When workers become interchangeable cogs in a machine, they come to feel that the only security for the individual lies in belonging to an organization of fellow workers.

What happened in Yankee City appears to have been happening throughout the country. With advances in technology and the development of big-city capitalism, the social distance between workers and management has been increasing, and we seem to be witnessing the emergence of an industrial working class.

The status of the worker has steadily deteriorated, and he has lost his chance to work his way up the craft ladder onto higher rungs of skill or into management. He has also lost the personal ties with management that might enable him to settle his grievances on an individual basis.

Since the workers are now sufficiently alike to have had common experiences and anxieties, it is no longer difficult for the industrial union to organize them into a group for collective bargaining. Besides exerting economic pressure, the union gives the workers a new sense of strength and becomes a powerful weapon to force management to recognize their worth as men. To compensate for their loss of status and for their anxieties in a changing industrial civilization, workers have been trying to find status and security in union organization.

American industry has been undergoing far-reaching changes in technology and human relations. It is only through an understanding of the nature of these changes in our way of life that it is possible to explain the labor strife that spreads through the cities and towns of America.

The Corporation Community

WILLIAM H. WHYTE, JR.

The previous selection concentrated on the effects of the nationally owned and controlled corporation on the social relations of a local New England community, especially on the resulting status insecurities at the lower levels of society. This selection looks at the same problem from a different angle. It analyzes the mobility patterns, family relations, and status strivings of the junior executives and their wives who are members of the postwar corporate world which first invaded Yankee City in the late 1920s. Here are the more energetic and ambitious sons of the Yankee Cities and Middletowns of the nation who have gone away to college, to the Harvard Business School or Wharton, and are now on their determined ways to the top layers of the executive-suite level. And, though they often dream of doing so, they can't go home again. For, as is suggested in this selection and as will be spelled out in more detail in the one following, the home town they once knew is no longer there—at least in any sociological or esthetic sense.

— ie. small town USA

THE MAN WHO LEAVES HOME IS NOT THE EXCEPTION IN AMERICAN society but the key to it. Almost by definition, the organization man is a man who left home and, as it was said of the man who went from the Midwest to Harvard, kept on going. There have always been people who left home, and the number of them is not decreasing but increasing—and so greatly that those who stay put in the home town are often as affected by the emigration as those who leave.

From William H. Whyte, Jr., *The Organization Man,* pp. 269–277. Copyright © 1956, by William H. Whyte, Jr. Reprinted by permission of Simon and Schuster, Inc. The material beginning on p. 47 from William H. Whyte, Jr., "The Wives of Management," in *Is Anybody Listening?* Reprinted from the October 1951 issue of *Fortune* Magazine by special permission; © 1951 Time Inc.

When a man moves from one place to another he is not necessarily moving socially. If we look at the figures for geographic mobility, however, we find that there is a rough connection between the two kinds of movement. Consider the relationship between the physical movement and age, education, and occupation. Men in the twenty-five-to-thirty-four age group are only 7.5 per cent of the total population, but they account for 12.4 per cent of the migration. The second characteristic is education: the more of it, the more mobility. If a man goes to college now, the chances are almost even that he won't end up in his home state. Recent census figures and *Time*'s study, *They Went to College,* indicate that the educational level is higher among migrants than nonmigrants, and the higher the educational level, the more intensive the migration. Only 27.3 per cent of high-school grads aged twenty-five to thirty-four, for example, were interstate migrants, versus 45.5 per cent of those who had had at least one year of college. Of those who worked their way through in a college outside their home state, 69 per cent don't come back. And for all college men, incidentally, the higher the grades, the more likely they are to move. Next, income. As the correlation with education would suggest, the more the mobility, the more one is likely to be in the higher income brackets. Census figures do not break down migration by income groups, but the experience of direct-mail people indicates that address changes are most frequent in the $5,000 and over bracket. There are also indications that address changes are becoming more frequent in this group. In 1953, 14.8 per cent of *Fortune*'s subscribers changed addresses during the year. In 1954, 16.6 per cent, and in 1955, 17.4 per cent.

Records of long-distance movers show the same concentration of organization people. The greatest single group of their clients—between 40 and 50 per cent—is composed of corporation people being transferred from one post to another (with the corporation directly paying the bill). If to this group are added government, Army and Navy people, and corporation people leaving one company for another, roughly three quarters of all moves are accounted for by members of large organizations.

These people confound the usual concepts of class. Some can be described as upper class, some middle class, but it is the horizontal grouping in which they come together that is more significant. It does not declass them; however muffled, the differences in family background between organization people will never be erased. But they will be superseded. When organization people speak of the boat they are all in together, it is the horizontal grouping they are describing. They assimilate one another, and the fact that they all left home can be more important in bonding them than the kind of home they left is in separating them.

The export movement that brings them together has become thoroughly basic to our society. It is no longer a case of the special boy who had to get out of town to cross the tracks to find an outlet for his energies; now as many as three quarters of the town's young college men may be in the same position. Where are they to go after college? Back home? Lawyers and doctors can, and the majority do; they are in the happy position of being able to go home, to keep professionally alert, and to make a good bit of money at the same time. But for the others, opportunity seems to be elsewhere—not just for the delivery boy who became an Air Force lieutenant, but for the young man on the Hill who's gone off to join Du Pont.

It is understandable that American literature has been so long fascinated with the small town revisited, or lost.[1] Those who have gone away think often of what they left behind and they are curiously ambiguous in their feeling of estrangement. In the case of the organization transients, they feel they sacrificed much and they often wonder if the gain has been worth it. Most of them came from reasonably prosperous homes, and when they look back they remember the support of the kinfolk and friends about, the reassuring solidity of grandfather's mansard-roof house, and the feeling that they were part of the group that counted. The family name, as they so often say in retrospect, *meant* something. No longer: local prestige, they well know, is not for export, and what is one town's upper-upper would be another's middle class.

In leaving this behind, however, the transients also draw solace. They have entered the heavyweight competition, and if they do not enter the arena exactly barehanded, they feel down deep that they have proved themselves just a little bit better than those who didn't. One of the great tacit bonds the transients share is a feeling, justifiable or not, that by moving they acquire an intellectual breadth that will forever widen the gap between them and their home towns.

"Dave and I have often thought about going back to East Wells," a successful young executive's wife explains. "It's a beautiful old New England town and we both had such happy times there. But all the people who had anything on the ball seem to have left. There are a few who took over their fathers' business, but the rest—I hate to sound so snobbish, but, dammit, I *do* feel superior to them." And they can never really go back. Once the cord is broken, a return carries overtones of failure. "I'm fed up with New York," says one executive, "but if I went back to Taylorston I know damned well they'd think my tail was between my legs."

[1] Recently, *Point of No Return,* by J. P. Marquand; *A Pride of Lions,* by John Brooks; *The View from Pompey's Head,* Hamilton Basso. Forerunners would include Thomas Wolfe's *You Can't Go Home Again,* Willa Cather's *A Lost Lady.*

Even if the chance of transfer sends them back they will be strangers. They might still be able to pick up the local prestige they may have inherited, but if they do, it will be at the risk of weakening their new, and now more important, organization ties. One junior executive explained it to me this way: "Because of this last transfer I'm back here, almost by accident, where I was born. It ought to be a setup; frankly, my family is as old guard around here as they come. Well, it's a lot of crap, sure, but I must say I get a good bit of pleasure knowing I can join the City Club and my boss can't. But it's damned privately I think about it. If I am going to go ahead in this organization, the people I've got to get along with are the office crowd, and don't think I wouldn't get the business if they started reading about me in the social columns." Says another, "It's odd. Here I've got a social position a lot of people would give a fortune to get, but the minute I joined the corporation I had to turn my back on it. We're sort of declassed, and as far as Amy and I are concerned, it is as if we weren't born here at all."

But perhaps the most important reason the transients can't go home is that they won't find it there if they do. It is not just the physical changes—the new sub-developments on the old golf course, the shopping-center strip just outside town, the new factory. As the young transients have left town, their opposite numbers from other towns have come in, and in many American communities there has been wholesale displacement from positions of power of the names that once "meant" something. Even in towns relatively untouched by urbanization the exodus of youth has left a vacuum the community itself cannot replenish. The venerable Newburyport of "Yankee City" fame is an example. With a population of about 15,000 at this moment, Newburyport has not shared at all the population growth that has affected almost every "normal" American community; physically, it is the Newburyport of the 1800s with the addition of relatively few modern buildings.

But there is considerable mobility. High-school records show that roughly 25 per cent of the graduating class do not return to Newburyport but instead go off to join the organization world, and in many cases this geographic movement represents social movement as well. Meanwhile, the old upper-upper families of the beautiful houses on High Street have been giving way here and there; one by one the old houses are being sold as old ladies with them pass on. (Several have been bought by executives brought into town by local companies.) Newburyporters are sad at some aspects of the slow disintegration of the eighteenth-century idyl, but they are not entirely hostile to the twentieth century. The Newburyport paper is a running stream of items about efforts of citizens to bring in new industry, and after a strenuous local debate they got enough land condemned to make a sort of industrial park. The great suburban trend has not hit them yet, but the new highway up from Boston is broad and flat.

For many towns the tensions have been strong. The new people may be a symbol of growth and prosperity, but much as resort natives view the "summer people" the old residents see them as something of a threat. These people and the corporation that is bringing them not only upset the historically low wage structure of the town, they have upset the whole local order of things. Whether his blood is blue or not, the general manager of the corporation's branch plant wields key power, and the townspeople know it. It is little wonder that corporations think long and hard about the tact of the proconsuls—and their wives—that they send to the far reaches of the empire.

Thus the pleasant young couple driving slowly along in their ranch wagon looking at the old houses can be to a somewhat dispossessed gentry a portent they fear. A member of one of the prominent families in one old town asked me, a comparative stranger, what were the people like that lived in the new houses on the hill across from her farm. "My husband and I are sick about it. We sold the twenty acres over there because we needed the money, but now look what's happened. Those ugly little boxes they're putting up! They cost like sin but there's not one in good taste. These people have no style at all. I wonder where Tom [president of a near-by steel company] finds them all. They are all bright, I suppose. Those wives with their silly babble and their middle-western twangs! They have already just about taken over the golf club, and now Charlie wants me to entertain some of them. I simply won't. I'll be pleasant to them, but they have their way and I have mine."

The newcomers can often sense the distaste. The transients may tell you about a wonderfully exceptional town they hit, but they are more likely to tell you of towns that proffered a cold shoulder. Sometimes they speak of outright antagonism on the part of the locals. If the community is one that has been expanding rapidly, the apprehensions over the newcomers can get translated very quickly into such matters as zoning and club restrictions, and the little developments that encircle some towns form what is in effect a ring of animosities.[2]

The same process of replacement has been going on, somewhat more painlessly, in the great metropolitan centers. Because of the greater

[2] A Study by New York University's Dr. Marie Jahoda indicates that in its initial stages of development, the people in Fairless Hills, Pennsylvania, believed that most of the other people in lower Bucks County disliked them. They were quite right.

number of opportunities it offers, one might assume that the city would much more easily use its home-grown talent to staff its institutions. Even here, however, the natives have been outnumbered by the newcomers. Philadelphia, for example, has long been considered quite inbred, yet a study by sociologist Digby Baltzell reveals that as early as 1940, 64 per cent of the Philadelphia business and professional leaders listed in *Who's Who* were born outside the Philadelphia area; in time, he documents, the influx of new blood in the positions of power is reflected in the Social Register.

The same process is going on everywhere. As the seats of economic power have shifted from the local, home-grown institutions to national organizations, membership in the elite of many a city or town is being determined less by hereditary ties, more by current functional rank. Not only are the national institutions sending in more people, the local institutions themselves are also being opened to outsiders more than before. The urban elite, in short, has become an ex-officio elite.

To document the facts of current mobility is not to furnish proof that it will continue, and I have met many who believe that in its present order of magnitude it is a temporary phenomenon. I think they underestimate the force of momentum in this respect. It is true enough that the postwar physical expansion of industry has been a great factor, and we cannot count on this as a constant. The more intangible aspects of mobility, however, can be just as important. Turnover has a way of begetting turnover, for as people become acclimated to current necessity there is a natural tendency to make it into a desirability.

Let me turn for a moment to corporation transfer policy, for it helps illuminate the self-perpetuating nature of the mobility. When the recruit joins up he does not do so because he *wants* to move a lot, and it is often in spite of it. But moving, he knows, has become part of the bargain, and unsettling as transfer might be, even more unsettling are the implications of not being asked to transfer. "We never plan to transfer," as one company president explains a bit dryly, "and we never make a man move. Of course, he kills his career if he doesn't. But we never *make* him do it." The fact is well understood; it is with a smile that the recruit moves—and keeps on moving—year after year, until, perhaps, that distant day when he is summoned back to Rome.

It is not just more moves per man. Even companies reporting no increase in the number of times each individual moves report an increase in the sheer number of men being moved. G. E. has compared a cross section of its forty-five-year-old executives with one of its thirty-five-year-olds. In the ten years after they were twenty-five, 42 per cent of the older group had moved at least once; during the same age period, 58 per cent of the younger had moved.

Corporations never planned it quite that way. Decentralization and expansion, rather than deliberate personnel policy, have determined the pattern. Companies have systematized it, to be sure. Moves are settling into more of a rhythm, and almost invariably they are sweetened by special departments that handle all the housekeeping fuss of the trip. By and large, however, the question of the man's personal development—however emphasized when the boss breaks the news to him—has been secondary to the day-to-day necessity of filling vacancies out in the empire.[3]

That is, up until now. Periodic transfer, some companies are coming to believe, is a positive good in itself; and even where no immediate functional reason exists, it might often be important to move the man anyway. What better way, they ask, to produce the well-rounded executive? Instead of leaving transfer to be determined haphazardly by different departments, some companies, like G.E., have made such decisions part of a systematic managerial program. By thus making a man's "permanent" assignment (i.e., one lasting at least three years) part of a deliberate rotation policy, the man is given "more choices in life to make," and the company, as a result, is given a pool of seasoned talent. Other companies agree. By deliberately exposing a man to a succession of environments, they best obtain that necessity of the large organization—the man who can fit in anywhere. "The training," as an I.B.M. executive succinctly puts it, "makes our men interchangeable."

And is not this the whole drift of our society? We are not interchange-

[3] There are still a number of environments, it should be noted, in which executives don't fit in—and some in which they fit in all too well. A good many companies have belatedly realized they have lost some of their best men by carelessly assigning them to San Francisco or Los Angeles for a spell. Even salary boosts often fail to achieve repatriation; once tested, the California way of life dulls such appetites—a fact that has sometimes been reflected in a salary differential between the West Coast and the East. When Shell Chemical moved its head office to New York from San Francisco some of its management group resigned rather than go along, and several who did go along eventually decided to go back. Another company recently located a lab on the Coast, it admits, mainly to hang onto talent it might otherwise lose.

On the other hand, there are some kinds of environments many people can't be tempted into trying at all. This has been particularly evident in the postwar moves of entire headquarters to the hinterlands. Making a small town a way station on the executive route is one thing; making it Mecca, another. An organization's creative and professional people usually will move permanently to a small town only if it is in striking distance of a large city and the professional contacts it affords. Similarly, almost any executive is likely to balk—for a while at least—if the town is so small that the influx of the company threatens a resurgence of the paternalistic company town.

able in the sense of being people without differences, but in the externals of existence we are united by a culture increasingly national. And this is part of the momentum of mobility. The more people move about, the more similar the American environments become, and the more similar they become, the easier it is to move about.

More and more, the young couples who move do so only physically. With each transfer the décor, the architecture, the faces, and the names may change; the people, the conversation, and the values do not—and sometimes the décor and the architecture don't either. If there are no company people to help the newcomers break the ice, there are almost bound to be some fellow transients near by, and the chances are good that some of them will be couples that the most recent arrivals have run into somewhere else in this great new freemasonry of transients. It is, they like to observe, a small world. "I just jump to read the new-arrivals list in the local paper," says a typical transient. "We've already run up against a couple from our Cambridge days at the Business School, and we're sure that some from Park Fairfax or Fresh Meadows will be along soon too." But even if they know no one it will not make too much difference. Whatever their respective organizations, they will share the same problems, the same kind of memories and aspirations. To use a favorite phrase, they talk the same language.

Where does the wife fit into all this? Individually, executives concede that her influence on the caste and social system of business is tremendous, and generally can tell some pretty hair-raising stories to prove it. Collectively, however, they find it almost too embarrassing to bring up, and official corporation policy, as a result, has tended in the past to treat this particular marriage of the executive as a sort of morganatic union—perfectly all right, but one best considered a rather private affair.

For the good of the corporation, many executives believe, it is time the matter was remedied. "We control a man's environment in business and we lose it entirely when he crosses the threshold of his home," one executive says mournfully. "Management, therefore, has a challenge and an obligation to deliberately plan and create a favorable, constructive attitude on the part of the wife that will liberate her husband's total energies for the job." Others, though they might not put it quite so badly, agree that the step is logical.

Just how to do this is a problem that has many a management understandably baffled. On one very basic matter, however, management is not in the slightest baffled. It knows exactly what kind of wife it wants. With a remarkable uniformity of phrasing, corporation officials all over the country sketch the ideal. In her simplest terms, she is a wife who is (1) highly adaptable, (2) highly gregarious, (3) realizes her husband belongs to the corporation.

Is the corporation asking the impossible? It would appear not. For the significant fact that emerges from any study of the question is not that corporations are trying to get this kind of wife. The significant fact is that they *are* getting her. If the wives of management are any criterion, our schools and colleges—and U.S. society in general—are producing the most tractable, system-minded youth we have ever had.

Let us define terms: we are discussing the wives of the coming generation of management, whose husbands are between twenty-five and forty, and in junior or middle management or with logical aspirations of getting there. There is, of course, no sharp dividing line between age groups, but among older executives there is a strong feeling that this younger generation of wives is the most cooperative the corporation has ever enlisted. "Somehow," says one executive, "they seem to give us so much less trouble than the older ones." "Either the girls are better or the men are marrying better," says another. "But whatever it is with these people, they get along."

Perhaps it is merely that this generation of wives has not yet grown older and more cantankerous. Perhaps. But there is evidence that this group-mindedness is the result of a shift in values more profound than one might suppose. It cannot be regarded as peculiar to the corporation wife, but by the nature of her job she may well be the outstanding manifestation of it. And a preview, perhaps, of what is to come.

Let us look first at how the wives themselves conceive their role. Critical literature has been answering the question rather forcefully, with the result that many Americans (and practically all Europeans) assume that the wife of the American businessman is not only the power behind the scenes but wants to become more so. The picture needs considerable revision. For the striking thing that emerges from wives' comments is the negativeness of the role they sketch. As they explain it, the good wife is good by *not* doing things—by *not* complaining when her husband works late; by *not* fussing when a transfer is coming up; by *not* engaging in any controversial activity. Moreover, they agree heartily that a good wife can't help a husband as much as a bad wife can hurt one. And the bad wife, clearly, is one who obtrudes too much—whether as a "meddler," a "climber," a "fixer," or, simply, someone who "pushes" her man around.

This conservatism is fairly recent. Slick-magazine fiction, that excellent index of accepted values, documents the shift. As late as the mid-thirties, a plot analysis indicates, stories were full of "dumb" smart girls, manipulating their amiable but often oafish husbands to business success.

No longer. In affairs of commerce today's heroines are lovable nitwits, while the husbands, with tousled hair and lopsided grin, definitely run the show. It is still, in short, a man's world.

So, at least, it is to the executive wife. Resolutely antifeminist, she conceives her role to be that of a "stabilizer"—the keeper of the retreat, the one who rests and rejuvenates the man for the next day's battle. "A man gets so frustrated at the office—it's such a rat race—he should be able to come home to calmness" . . . "You make it so he can relax" . . . "I try to see that there aren't any problems left around the house."

This stabilizing calls for more than good homemaking and training the kids not to bother Daddy before dinner. Above all, wives emphasize, they have to be good listeners. They describe the job somewhat wryly—they must be "sounding boards," "refueling stations," "wailing walls"—but they speak without resentment. Nurturing the male ego, they seem to feel, is not only a pretty good fulfillment of their own ego but a form of therapy made increasingly necessary by the corporation way of life. Management psychologists couldn't agree more. "Most top executives are very lonely people," as one puts it. "The greatest thing a man's wife can do is to let him unburden the worries he can't confess to in the office."

In addition to listening, she can do some judicious talking. If she is careful about it, she can be a valuable publicity agent for the husband. "In a subtle way," says one executive, "they put in a plug for the husband, they tell things he wouldn't dare tell for fear of seeming immodest." In similar fashion they can humanize him if he's a boss. "About the time I get fed up with the bastard," says a junior executive, "here I am, going over to dinner at his house. And she's so nice—she jokes about him, kids him to his face—I figure he can't be so bad after all."

Good, low-key "stabilizing," then, the wife sees as her main task. There is another aspect to her role, however, and it is a good bit less passive. For the good corporation wife must also be a social operator—and when husbands and wives sketch out the personal characteristics of the ideal wife it is the equipment for this role that comes first to their minds. What they ask for, more than any other quality, is gregariousness—or a reasonable facsimile. Here are some of the ways in which they spell it out.

> EXECUTIVE: "She should do enough reading to be a good conversationalist . . . Even if she doesn't like opera she should know something about it, so if the conversation goes that way she can hold her own. She has to be able to go with you if you're going to make a speech or get an award, and not be ill at ease."

EXECUTIVE: "The hallmark of the good wife is the ability to put people at their ease."

WIFE: "The most important thing for an executive's wife is to know everybody's name and something about their family so you can talk to them—also, you've got to be able to put people at their ease."

EXECUTIVE: "Keeping herself so she is comfortable with people on the boss's level is important. I don't think reading and music and that kind of stuff are vital."

EXECUTIVE: "The kind you want is the kind that can have people drop in any time and make a good show of it even if the baby's diapers are lying around."

WIFE: "It's a very worth-while bunch we have here. Edith Sampson down on Follansbee Road is sort of the intellectual type, but most of the gang are real people."

For the corporation wife, in short, being "sociable" is as important as stabilizing. Like the Army wife (an analogy she detests), she must be a highly adaptable "mixer." In fact, she needs to be even more adaptable than the Army wife, for the social conditions she meets are more varied. One year she may be a member of a company community, another year a branch manager's wife, expected to integrate with the local community, or, in some cases, to become a civic leader; and frequently, as the wife of the company representative, to provide a way station on the route of touring company brass.

As a rule, she is inextricably bound up in the corporation "family," often so much so that her entire behavior—including what and where she drinks—is subtly conditioned by the corporation. "It makes me laugh," says one wife in an Eastern city dominated by one corporation. "If we were the kind to follow The Pattern, I'll tell you just what we would do. First, in a couple of years, we'd move out of Ferncrest Village (it's really pretty tacky there, you know). We wouldn't go straight to Eastmere Hills—that would look pushy at this stage of the game; we'd go to the hilly section of Scrubbs Mill Pike. About that time, we'd change from Christ Church to St. Edwards, and we'd start going to the Fortnightlys—it would be a different group entirely. Then about ten years later, we'd finally build in Eastmere Hills." That would be the signal, she believes, that they had moved into the top-brass bracket. "It just makes me laugh," she says, happily.

Few wives are as articulate as that on the social role, but intuitively they are generally superb at it; their antennae are sensitive, and the rules of the game they know by heart. Second nature to the seasoned wife, for example, are the following:

Don't talk shop gossip with the Girls, particularly those who have husbands in the same department.
Don't invite superiors in rank; let them make the first bid.
Don't turn up at the office unless you absolutely have to.
Don't get too chummy with the wives of associates your husband might soon pass on the way up.
Don't be disagreeable to any company people you meet. You never know . . .
Be attractive. There is a strong correlation between executive success and the wife's appearance—particularly so in the case of the sales wife.
Be a phone pal of your husband's secretary.
Never—repeat, never—get tight at a company party (it may go down in a dossier).

One rule transcends all others: *Don't be too good.* Keeping up with the Joneses is still important; but where in pushier and more primitive times it implied going substantially ahead of the Joneses, today keeping up means just that: keeping up. One can move ahead, yes—but slightly, and the timing must be exquisite. "We will have a grand piano," says one wife, "when we are ready for it"—which is quite different from "when we can afford it." Whatever the move, it must never be openly invidious. Perhaps it is for this reason that the Buick is such a preferred car; it envelops the whole executive spectrum and the jump from a Special to a Super, and from a Super to a Roadmaster, can be handled with tact.

Neither must one be too outstanding in more personal ways. The good corporation wife does not make her friends uncomfortable by clothes too blatantly chic, references to illustrious forebears, or excessive good breeding. And intellectual pretensions she avoids like the plague. It is interesting to watch one wife rearrange her magazine basket as she primps for callers; almost automatically, she shuffles her *Harper's* and *Atlantic Monthly* beneath the pile. The Girls might not understand.

Are these rules of the game merely the old fact of conformity? In part, yes. But something new has been added. What was once a fact has now become a philosophy. Where people used to like to talk, at least, of "individualism," today's young couples are without hypocrisy on the matter; not only do they concede their group-mindedness, they are outspoken in favor of it. They blend with the group not because they fear to do otherwise, but because they approve of it.

The net effect is more than the mere Babbittry young couples' frankness so often makes it sound. A "real" person, the wife explains, is one "who thinks of other people." Her search for fulfillment, to be sure, includes popularity but it also includes civic activities, P.T.A., and all the intangible satisfactions of *esprit de corps*. Even her tensions are in character; for it is almost an article of faith with her that her deepest personal desires and the values of the group contain no conflict that a little "adjusting" can't fix up—and it does not, unfortunately, always work out that way.

The corporation itself has a way of exploding her equable world. On one very crucial question, as a result, the rules of the game contain an inconsistency that can pose for the wife a wrenchingly tough dilemma. *What is she to do if her husband begins moving up faster than his age group?* In advancing the husband in the office, the corporation is quite likely to advance him socially as well; it may, for example, put him up for membership (when the company quota opens up) in one of the better local clubs; or suggest to him that just by the way there happens to be a good real-estate bargain in a suburb favored by the brass.

There is no easy way for the couple in such cases, and for the wife the inward tug of war between the social status quo and the prospect of advancement can be extremely poignant. As one young executive puts it, "If I go ahead as I hope, and some of our friends progress as little as I think they will, there's going to be friction. My wife can't see this. She thinks we'll hold them as friends; she is nice to everyone and thinks if you are that way, everyone will be nice to you."

The shock is not long in coming. "I must have made some terrible mistakes," laments one wife now in midpassage. "I love people and I've made many intimate friends in the company, but since Charlie got his new job it's just been hell on us. He has so much control over their lives, and it's gotten so complicated." In a larger community the ascendant couple would have recourse, for there exists a sort of freemasonry of success, where they can talk freely without anyone taking offense. But in the smaller community their upward course is more difficult, as, baffled and hurt, they try to hang on to their old friends and wonder why they are rebuffed.

Eventually most adjust. The price, however, is a kind of social professionalism. The wife must now learn to make "constructive" friendships, to become consciously aware of the vagaries and gradations of the social structure of business—and learn to play an entirely new role in it. "It's tough," says the wife of a thirty-five-year-old plant manager. "You have got to leave behind your old friends. You have to weigh the people you invite to parties. You have to be careful of who you send Christmas cards to and who you don't. It sounds like snobbery, but it's just something you have to do. You have to be a boss's wife."

While few young wives are aware of the sacrifice involved, the role of the boss's wife is one that they very much covet. In talking about the qualities of the ideal wife—a subject they evidently had thought over long and often—they were at no loss. In one-third of the cases, the word "gracious" came instantly to them, and in nearly all the others the descriptions amounted to the same thing. Theirs is a sort of First Lady ideal, a woman who takes things as they come with grace and poise, and a measure of *noblesse oblige;* in short, the perfect boss's wife.

So far, not so difficult for the wife. In respect to her outward, social role, at least, she can reflect that there is no conflict that some good, hard adjusting can't fix up. But is the same true of her more basic role—helpmate to the husband? As psychiatrists know only too well, the role of the perfect wife she so skillfully affects to herself is something of an illusion.

What, for example, of the listening job that wives take such pride in? How well *can* they listen? They bring certain natural interests to the job; they are extremely interested in the husband's salary, in his status—often, indeed, more than he is himself—and they have the normal feminine curiosity for human relationships. And though the details interest them much less, most realize that they should have a grasp of the husband's responsibilities.

Yet, granted all this, how much do they know about their husbands' work? Consensus of a cross section of U.S. executives: very little. ("And for God's sake, don't quote me.") Some wives are notable exceptions, but the dinner conversations sketched by most executives run a highly similar course. When office politicking is involved, the lady's interest perks, and the husband who has just been chewed out by the boss can get understanding because she listened well when he told her before what a jerk the boss was. But the husband who has spent the day sweating out more involved problems gets no such solace ("she just gets restless and changes the subject"); and those that have to wrestle with tough technical problems get almost none for the simple reason that their wives haven't the faintest idea of what they are talking about.

The wives get the blame—and many accept it. After the first blush of interest has worn off, some concede they can muster so little curiosity in the details of their husband's work that their listening becomes progressively more passive. There are excuses aplenty. "If he has had a rough day," says one wife, "I don't want to hear about it. He'd only get mad and say things the children shouldn't hear." "I suppose I'm a little bit of a moral coward," says another, "after about ten minutes of listening, I find it so convenient to turn to the children and answer their questions instead."

The husband, however, may be the one chiefly to blame. He asks for active, intelligent listening, yet seldom wants advice ("She always sees everything in black and white" . . . "jumps to conclusions every time" . . . "women just don't understand"). More important, he has neither the patience nor the inclination to give his wife the exposition necessary for understanding. "It's like taking a girl to a baseball game," explains one executive. "You want her to understand the game, but you get so damned tired of her silly questions."

The baseball analogy is a little one-sided. There is another reason for the husband's reticence. Even to his wife he instinctively presents something of a doctored self-image—and as the old saw about valets goes, it is not something to stand too brilliant a light. "Automatically, we build ourselves up to them," concedes one executive. "It all comes back to the fact, I guess, that mentally anyway you really want her to stay the hell at home."

Like the coal mines in which woman must never set foot, the office can spell sanctuary. And the fact does not go unresented. "It's as if," says one wife, "he lived twice as much as I." Perhaps this is why the Christmas office party provokes such surprisingly bitter, if concealed, feeling from many wives. It dramatizes the wife's exclusion. Here, on this appointed day, is the world she can never share, and for all her brave little chuckles at the standing jokes of the office gang, she comes face to face with the fact. That is, if she's allowed to attend.

Burning though this exclusion may be to the wives, it is a topic they dislike intensely to talk about—or to think about. And for them, indeed, the waters may well be better left muddy: to peer too deeply is to uncover an underlying point even more provoking. Where, the awful question comes up, does the man find his major satisfactions?

A common feminine observation is that, of course, the man's major satisfactions come from the home; if he's happy there, why, then he can be happy in his work—and if he is happy in his work, then he is happy in his home, too. The belief is probably necessary. Is it correct as well?

Item: If the home is the executive's end-all, why has he become a defaulting father? As an earlier *Fortune* survey (August, 1946) indicates, the husband wants to turn over more of the child rearing to the wife than she is willing to assume.

One of the most general plaints of executives' wives is summed up in a sentence: he doesn't spend enough time with the kids. In most cases, the husbands agree; if only it weren't for the treadmill . . .

Item: As management psychologists note, the average executive shows a remarkable ability to repress his home worries while on the job; rarely, however, can he shut out office worries at home.

Item: The downright fright of many executives at the prospect of imminent retirement. Here would seem to be the fulfillment of all he has worked for. Why, then, does he view it with such dismay?

Item: The reaction to this Hobson's choice question: "If you had to make the choice, which would you take: an increasingly satisfying work life and a proportionately souring home life—or the opposite?" The answers would surprise wives. "This business of doing it all for the family," as one husband confesses, "it's just a rationalization. If I got a windfall today I'd still knock myself out." Even those who duck the question do so on the grounds that one alternative is not realistic. They simply can't conceive, they say, of a home life being happy if the job isn't.

"Man's love is of man's life a thing apart," Byron once observed. " 'Tis woman's whole existence." So, for all the group integration and communication skills she can muster, it will probably remain.

The schism between Home and Office does not remain subterranean. Inevitably, it comes to the surface on those infrequent but critical occasions when the husband and wife must weigh the question of ambition. In the earlier days the task would have been less ticklish for them; ambition was then conceived of in terms of definite, concrete goals—like making half a million, perhaps, on building the biggest skyscraper. Now, however, ambition has become relative; it floats in space and time, fixed only by the progress of the group. The young couple are no less ambitious than their predecessors, but they see no sense in constructing definite goals, what with taxes, war threats, and such; furthermore, they want to be team players, and ambition too graphic would be no help.

The effect of this double drive is a dilemma. Reduced to its simplest terms it runs like this: I want to take it easy, I want to enjoy life and yet I want to keep up. But since everyone else wants to—and we can't get together—we all end up knocking ourselves out. Thus the high frequency in the talk of younger executives of words like "treadmill," "twirl," "whirlpool," "rat race," "merry-go-round," all implying a futile perpetual motion. In counterpoint, they speak, wistfully, of settling on a "plateau" instead of continuing the climb—there is almost the suggestion of how wonderful it would be if everyone could just get together in a sort of cartel agreement on ambition. But the executive knows better; he'll never get promoted unless he's something of a rate buster, and rate busters can't park on The Plateau. The "antagonistic cooperation," to use David Riesman's phrase, must continue.

Here we come to the misunderstanding. The wife believes in The

Plateau. The more philosophic wives see man's drive and ambition as the core of his being; a lot talk that way, but most see man's drive as an unnecessarily divisive factor in the home. For the security that so preoccupies wives includes not only a good income, but a husband still alive and reasonably kicking at fifty. And the immediate consequences can be as important. Says one industrial psychologist: "I've had a number of executives whose job effectiveness is impaired because they are sexually frustrated. It is possible that these men have drained off their energy through worry over the job so much they are no longer any good as lovers. This makes them worry even more. One excellent man I've had to study is losing his grip fast. His wife's an outgoing, attractive gal that now finds him lacking sexually. She's now practically an alcoholic."

Whatever the specters—coronary thrombosis, impotence, nervous breakdowns—the wife worries about them as much as if not more than the husband who may be afflicted. They bar the way to The Plateau, and it is a dream she never stops cherishing. For good reason, the "bad wives" she speaks of are not the wives who hold down their husbands but those who push them—the wives, in other words, who upset the applecart.

But it is the corporation that wives see as chiefly to blame—and it is only in this respect that they exhibit any real animus toward it. Since the husband works largely for the goal of a happy home, they reason, his overwork must be due to the pressure put on him by the corporation. "There must be something wrong with industry," says one wife. "My husband doesn't think he's overworking, but he is. They must make him." With a wealth of unsettling detail, wives paint the picture of a corporation consuming their men.

It is the wife's duty, it follows, to offset this pressure with counterpressure of her own. This she does incessantly. "I've let Bob know I would sooner have him in a lower job than knocking himself out as a v.p." . . . "When Edgar's work gets so it's interfering with his health and happiness, it's not worth it. I keep telling him we're a lot better off than most—another car and things like that aren't necessary." . . . "He probably won't make the Executive Committee, and I don't want him to. It would take all of him—and what good would the extra money be then?" So, over countless dinner tables, is the sermon preached.

How effective is the sermon? In some cases it has held a husband back, for it has influenced him in one of those vital fork-in-the-road decisions. In the average case? "I'll tell you what good it does," says one executive. "Every tenth time I listen." Others agree; the badgering sometimes does have a valuable braking effect. As one man puts it, "If the wife doesn't put pressure on you to be home on the five-thirty, and the company wants you around, it's hard to back away from the office."

Unfortunately, however, the braking effect is severely limited by one simple fact. The wife constantly visualizes the cost of ambition; rarely, however, does she visualize the social cost of the lack of it. You cannot get to be a boss's wife, unfortunately, unless your husband gets to be a boss, and when the couple have to get down to cases the inconsistency blows up in her face. "The minute you put the dollar sign on your work," says one husband, "she gets ambitious quick." And again, the group resolves the problem; as another husband puts it, "If my wife gabs to you as she does to me about settling for what we have now—well, just ask her which one of her friends' husbands she would take as my boss."

In this problem of ulcers and ambition the corporation has been, at worst, no more than an exacerbating influence. It is ironic, therefore, that the wives rest their case against it on the ground of pressure. For there is one way in which the corporation has become an active, if involuntary, agent of the division—and it is something quite different from what the wives suspect.

Thanks, in part, to the way the tax structure has accumulated, the corporation now provides the man with a higher standard of living in his work than in his home—and, it might be added, a higher one than his wife enjoys. From nine to five he may be a minor satrap, guiding the destiny of thousands, waited on by secretaries and subordinates; back in his servantless home, he washes the dishes. Nor is it merely the fact of his satrapy; the corporation virtually rigs it so that he can have more fun away from home.

The expense account has become a way of life. There is not only travel, there are luncheon clubs, company retreats, special conventions, parties, and perquisites, and though the wife may be thrown an occasional convention as a crumb, the expense-account world rarely encompasses her. It is primarily a man's world—and if the man is at a low salary, he is likely to find the pattern of life at 7118 Crestmere Road dull in comparison.

"The company has spoiled Jim terribly," says one wife. "Even when he was only earning $7,500 a year, he used to be sent to Washington all the time. He'd go down in a Pullman drawing room and, as J. R. Robinson of the General Company, take a two-room suite. Then he used to be asked by some of the company officers to a hunting and fishing lodge that the company kept in the north woods. When he went to New York, he'd entertain at 21, the Barberry Room, and the Chambord. Me, meanwhile, I'd be eating a 30-cent hamburger and when we went away together on vacation, we would have to go in our beat-up old car, or borrow my sister's husband's. This taste of high life gives some of these characters delusions of grandeur. Small wonder that they get to fidgeting after they have been home a couple of weeks."

Curiously, the disparity does not exercise most wives, or to put it another way, what they don't know doesn't hurt them. Of the wives interviewed, many mentioned, commiseratingly, how their husbands looked forward to coming home, how awful it was sleeping in hotel beds, rattling around on trains, and eating bum food. "What the hell can you say?" says one executive. "Here I am eating high off the hog, meeting interesting people, while Jo is slaving back home. I get a big bang out of all this, but I also have a sort of guilty feeling, so I say to her, 'Gee, honey, I hate all this traveling, but I just have to do it.' "

There are some things, however, that cannot be explained away. For more than sirloins and drawing rooms are at issue; over the long pull this disparity aggravates perhaps the most subtle problem of marriage: equality of growth. If marriage, as sociologist Everett Hughes puts it, is a "mutual mobility bet," for whom are the cards stacked?

Growth can mean many things; to the younger generation of executives it seems to mean an increasing ability to handle and mix with people. And the terms are the same for the wife. "The wife who is not very sociable," goes a highly typical male observation, "might not affect the husband directly, but she can hurt him just the same. A lot of business is done week ends. If she doesn't go for this, her lack of growth can hold the man back." Even the old idea of a wife as a sort of culture carrier is virtually dead; she is still expected to read and things like that, but for functional reasons. "Sure I want her to read good books and magazines," as one executive puts it, "I don't want her to make a fool of herself in conversation."

By this yardstick of growth, the corporation virtually forces the progress of the man. But what, meanwhile, is happening to the wife? "We give our young men finish and finesse because we give them an opportunity to observe men who are ahead of them," one company head points out. "We do nothing for the wife." Significantly, she rarely worries over the fact. Husbands do. In most cases they seem well enough satisfied; they speak often of a pause in her growth that occurs with the birth of the first child and continues until the children are well into junior high. But, they observe, leisure time opens up once again and she can catch up.

But there is another pattern, too. Though it is much more infrequent, it is one that corporations find anguishing because it is highlighted by the very potential of the man. "I have seen it happen so many times," says one executive, sadly. "He marries the kid sweetheart, the girl next door, or a girl from the jerkwater college he went to. They start off with a lot in common—but then he starts going up. Fifteen years later he is a different guy entirely; he dresses differently, talks differently, thinks differently. But she's stayed home—literally and figuratively."

The pattern is particularly acute with the corporations that draw their executive material from the ranks. Says a personnel man of a large retail organization, "It's a classic problem with us; a clerk marries the salesgirl at the notions counter. Ten years later we may be ready to make him a store manager in a locality where he has to move in country-club circles and uphold a certain position in the town—a store manager has to relate the store to the community. Some of the wives never can seem to do this. An awful lot of unhappiness comes out of it."

The effect on the marriage is profound. If the wife defends herself by enveloping her husband with home ties, he is put at an intolerable disadvantage in competing with his less enveloped associates. Some husbands subside and try to enjoy it. Most seek escape. For them the office becomes the spiritual home, the house merely a base of operations, and the wife somebody to be kept in the background lest one's style be cramped. The effect on her? She does not always immolate herself in the home; companionship, sometimes alcoholic, is to be had with other such wives—often you may see her at the club, idly plunking quarters into the slot machines. The proportion of alcoholism among upper management wives is not a verifiable statistic, but the extraordinary amount of behind-the-scenes concern about it in different companies suggests it is much higher than is generally supposed.

While the socially retarded wife has become the secret sorrow of the corporation, and partly its responsibility, there is little it believes it can do. Most corporations keep tabs on the wife's growth only as an index to the executive's availability for certain positions. As a result, the topic is generally not brought up until events force it.

It is time, some executives think, that young men were frankly told about the problem. "I generally warn the younger men," says one company president, "of this danger of their wives' not keeping up with them. I suggest to them that they encourage their wives to join things, to play golf, to go on business trips with them occasionally." Many have been grateful for the advice. Says one rapidly climbing executive, "I have let my wife know that she must grow with me. Sometimes there has been a problem as to who was to baby-sit when there was a community meeting. I have told her that I would stay at home—it was more important for her to go. And I think I've learned it earlier than most."

Is the moral that he should marry a girl "superior" to him? Thanks to the commonly accepted saw that a woman can pull a man up, but not vice versa, there are many who think he should. ("My best executives," remarks one boss, "are the ones who 'outmarried' themselves.") But the pitfalls are many. Her qualities may drive the man to preoccupation with office prestige in order to prove himself to her; furthermore, unless she is excellent at hiding her superiority—or lets it rest fallow—she can hurt his chances in a close "family" community. The Bryn Mawr accent can be absolute death for a career in some Midwest corporations.

What kind of background for the woman, then, is the optimum? A serious career can be dismissed easily; there is almost universal agreement among wives, husbands, and corporations on this score. Work before marriage, however, is generally approved. "I feel the fact that I worked before marriage," says one wife, "is a help. I know what goes on in an office and can understand what Charles is up against."

College? Here is the *summum bonum*. There are some obvious reasons; because virtually all executives now go to college, the couple in such cases start off with shared values. But corporation people mention a reverse factor almost as much. It is not so important for the wife, they say, to have gone to college; but it is very important not to have *not* gone to college. If she hasn't, corporation people warn, she is prey to an inferiority complex that makes it difficult for her to achieve real poise. Some corporations, accordingly, make it their business to find out whether or not the wife has a degree.

In this respect, the corporation would seem to have reason for optimism. Since more girls are going to college now, the proportion of executives' wives who are college graduates has been steadily increasing. Partly as a result of this, other executives feel, the problem of the outgrown wife appears to be diminishing. And they see other good omens as well. Rarely has there emerged a generation of wives so dedicated to the job of adjustment. On almost every point of contact—from entertaining to moving across the continent—the wives' background is making them the most tractable material the corporation has ever had.

The Natural History of a Reluctant Suburb

WILLIAM M. DOBRINER

This essay combines a historical with an analytical approach to the social problems faced by Old Harbor, a once small and isolated village which is now part of the New York metropolitan area. It shows how Old Harbor was first invaded by wealthy members of the Gilded Age generation who built large estates there in the late nineteenth century; and how it has, since World War II, been struggling to keep its identity in spite of a new invasion of white-collar nomads, shopping centers, and expressways. It is important for the reader to see how the problems of Old Harbor are related to those discussed in the preceding selections. Thus Professor Dobriner, like De Grazia, Warner and Lowe, and Whyte, is interested in showing how changing social relationships influence attitudes and values. The old-timers, for example, have attitudes toward education very different from those of the newcomers to Old Harbor; and the differences reflect the underlying contrast between local and transcommunal loyalties which was discussed in the Introduction to this book. The contrast appears again in the following comments by two Old Harborites:

OLD TIMER: "I have traveled a lot in this country and I've been to Europe a couple of times too. But the biggest thrill in my life was when I got back from Europe and drove over Potter's Hill and saw the spire of Old First Church down in the valley. . . . I really love this town—Old Harbor is the finest community in the United States."

From William M. Dobriner, "The Natural History of a Reluctant Suburb," *The Yale Review* (Spring, 1960), pp. 399–412. Copyright, Yale University Press.

EXECUTIVE NOMAD: "I can't think of Old Harbor as my own town or anything like that. Most of my friends live closer to the city and I work there. I don't have any feeling of living in a small community or anything like that. I guess I sleep more of my time here than anything else. . . ."

ONE OF THE MOST PERSISTENT MISTAKES IN THE FLOOD OF LITerature about suburbia is the tendency to lump together under the label of "suburban" all sorts of communities caught within the cultural and economic shadow of great cities. But in fact there is an enormous difference between an all-new suburb like a Levittown and an established rural village invaded by suburbanites and turned into a reluctant suburb.

The internal problems of the mass-produced suburb and the sacked village are quite different. A Levittown has to create its institutions—its schools, its churches, its civic organization, shopping centers, "culture" groups, and the like. The invaded village, on the other hand, is a going concern before the suburban assault begins. It has evolved a social system that works for a population of a certain size. There are enough schools, churches, clubs, stores, streets, sewers, sidewalks, parking spaces, etc., to go around. But once the restless city discovers the little village and pumps a stream of suburbanites into its institutions, the social system soon develops a split personality. Where a Levittown is faced with the problem of creating a community from scratch, the sacked village has a community already, but it is soon divided between the pushy, progressive, and plastic world of the newcomers on the one hand, and the accustomed world of the oldtimers—"the villagers"—on the other.

Wherever the suburban spearhead is pressing the rural village, the village has little hope of surviving unchanged, because the forces behind metropolitan expansion are irresistible. For a while the village may resist by elaborate zoning requirements or other legal barriers to invasion, but these are at best delaying actions. The tides of urbanism may be diverted for a decade or so, but what direct assault has failed to do a fifth column will accomplish. The city will seduce the young people of the village; they will go to urban colleges, take jobs in the metropolis, extend their range of contacts and eventually adopt an urban (suburban) way of life.

What it means for a long-established village to be suburbanized can be seen from the recent history of a community called here, for reasons of tact, "Old Harbor." It is a real place, in the general New England area, off the Atlantic Coast. Over 300 years old, Old Harbor lies at the foot of a curving valley between two green necks of land stretching into the sea. Its history resembles that of many another New England village. In 1662, for example, a "morals committee" of six "respectable" citizens and the minister carefully scrutinized all new settlers who arrived in the community. If the newcomers failed to pass the committee's standards of morality and respectability, they were asked to leave. So Old Harbor's tradition of skepticism and caution as to the worth of recent arrivals is anchored in over 300 years of experience.

In its early years, Old Harbor served as the local nexus of an agrarian and colonial society. Its grist mills ground local grain into flour through the power of the impounded waters of the tide ponds and mill dams. The natural harbor drew shipping from all over the east coast. Whaling ships worked out of the home port, and coastal shipping from ports as far away as the West Indies unloaded hides, rum, cattle, cord-wood, charcoal, etc., on Old Harbor's busy wharfs. Over the years the farmers worked the land on the gently rolling slopes leading down to the water. The wheelwrights turned their wheels, the metal smiths pounded out their pewterware, the shipbuilders sent their vessels splashing into the bay, and the carpenters built the "saltbox" cottages down near the harbor. The village prospered but remained comparatively changeless in some fundamental ways—it continued to be a Yankee village of industrious merchants, seamen, farmers, and crafstmen. Certain family names appear again and again in its records: the Rodgerses, the Platts, the Tituses, the Woodses, the Brushes, the Conklins, the Wickses, the Scudders, the Sopers, the Skidmores. In time more land was cleared, more ships were built, and small but vigorously independent men set up industries and crafts, farms and homes. Yet the essential "ethos" of the village remained constant—Yankee, Protestant, independent, cautious, shrewd, calculating, hard-working, and conservative.

Old Harbor figured in the American Revolution. One of its churches (still standing and functioning) served as headquarters for the local British forces. Eventually, George Washington came to Old Harbor and slept there. By the middle of the nineteenth century, in a society where so many persons, traditions, and things were new, Old Harbor had a lineage of 200 years to look back upon. But change was imminent. In 1867 the railroad came to the village and became a serious competitor with marine transportation, and thereafter the harbor declined as a vital force in the village's economy. Even more ominous was the fact that 36.6 miles from the village lay the borders of a city. By today's standards, it was an urban infant, but even then it was showing a capacity for incredible growth and its influence was extending beyond its borders. Though it was still an entity apart and a universe removed from Old Harbor, some of the more perceptive villagers looked to "the city" with something more than casual Yankee curiosity and superiority. In writing to a relative in 1872, one villager noted, "There has been a very curious thing this summer, I must have seen 15 or 20 strangers in town during July and August."

The first invaders of Old Harbor were members of the new industrial aristocracy who emerged in the decades after the Civil War. They were the first outsiders to discover the magical little coves and their verdant overcover, the unspoiled woodlands, the tiny village with so much history, and the green, gentle hills with the spectacular sweep of the sea. By the turn of the century, Old Harbor had become their carefully guarded preserve. They bought the old farms and cleared away acres for their summer playgrounds and gigantic estates. They fenced off two- and three-hundred-acre parcels and created separate dukedoms populated by communities of servants and laborers.

On the surface things had not changed much. The rolling hills, the snug harbor, the Yankee village with its saltbox cottages and local crafts, the busy farms, all remained the same. The estates were secluded behind acres of greenery and the new leisure class strove to protect "the colonial charm" of the village and its surroundings. The old inhabitants kept to themselves. They ran the village as they always had, but supplied the estates with provisions, ships, and such services as they were capable of providing. Though there was little basic understanding and compatibility between the "high society" of the nation and the "high society" of the village, the coming of the estates brought a new prosperity to Old Harbor and helped to take up the slack left by the decline of the fishing and whaling industries and the harbor in general. By the turn of the century, Old Harbor was passing into another stage of its life. By now the grist mills were great sway-backed structures rotting by the mill dams. The brickkilns, the tannery, and Ezra Prime's thimble factory were alive only in the memories of the very old. Children played sea games in the soft, pungent, peeling hulks of the whalers as they lay beached in the harbor marshes, their masts pointing like splayed fingers against the evening sky. And in the meantime, to the east, the urban Goliath was yawning and stretching and looking fitfully about.

By the early 1920's, the township in which Old Harbor is located was undergoing rather intensive immigration from the metropolitan area. The city was going through one of its growth spasms, and the population was spilling over the city limits into the adjacent counties. Old Harbor was one county removed, but this was the decade in which the automobile drastically changed the character of American society and culture. Mass production had made Henry Ford's dream of a low-priced car for every family almost a reality. And a few miles to the south of the Village, in "Old Harbor Station," the railroad terminus, a new and rather singular figure stood on the platform waiting for the 8:05 to the city: the commuter, the classic suburbanite, with his freshly pressed tight trousers, starched white collar, and morning paper folded neatly under his arm.

Now the automobile and the new concrete highways were bringing transient strangers to Old Harbor. The strangers were noisily evident on hot summer nights when a two-hour drive would carry them from the heat and congestion of the city to the beaches and cool valleys of Old Harbor. The character of Old Harbor weekends rudely changed as streams of cranky autos on spindly wheels rattled through the center of town and jammed up at traffic lights. Not only was Main Street becoming a thoroughfare for the beach traffic on weekends, but the city people intruded into the private bathing places along the waterfront. "Private Property" and "No Admittance" signs began to obliterate "the view." The number of both permanent residents and weekend transients, or, as the villagers called them, "shoe boxers," increased.

By the 1930's, the age of the palatial estates, begun seventy-five years earlier, was about over. The huge mansions in English Tudor, Renaissance, Baroque, Spanish, and various combinations had served their purpose. They had proclaimed the grandeur of American industrial growth and had bestowed calculated and lavish honor on those who built them. Now they were in the hands of the third generation or had been sold to second and third buyers, and each time a portion of the land had been sliced off in the transaction. In addition, government action unfriendly to the rich in the New Deal decade was making it difficult to maintain huge houses; income and inheritance taxes were forcing the estate holders to sell their property or simply to let the palaces go to seed. A few were given to educational institutions and one or two more were turned over to Old Harbor Township as museums or public parks. But there is little contemporary use for a decaying 30-room castle with its entourage of outbuildings, so they waste away in their crabgrass kingdoms, the gargantuan headstones of an excessive age.

After the Second World War population that had been trapped in the city during the war years exploded into the county neighboring Old Harbor. In ten years, the number of people in this "rural" county passed a million and made it one of the most rapidly growing areas in the United States. Large numbers also spilled over into Old Harbor's county, whose sociological border by 1950 was well within the rural-urban fringe. In the ten years from 1945 to 1955, Old Harbor Township doubled its population, and the village itself has now absorbed between two and three times the numbers it had in 1940. In just ten years, a 300-year-old village, with many of the descendants of the original founders still living there, underwent a social shock that wrenched it from whatever remained of the patterns of the past.

As Old Harbor soaks up the steady stream of suburban migrants, it has taken on a physical pattern quite different from the community of twenty years ago. Toward the center of town is the "old village," the nucleus of the "old-timer" community. There the streets are lined with aging oaks, elms, and maples. The houses are comparatively large and reflect the architectural trends of 150 years—authentic and carefully preserved saltboxes and Cape Cods, two-story clapboard or brick Colonials, straight and angular American Gothics, and prissy, frivolous Victorians. They stand fairly close to each other, but property lines are marked by mature hedges of privet, forsythia, and weigelia. Each house proclaims an identity of its own. In front of an occasional Colonial or cottage a small sign will read "1782" or "1712." In the old village, even on a sunny day, there is shade and the scent of many carefully tended flowers. The sunlight filters through the great overhead branches and throws delicately filigreed shafts of yellow-green light on the clipped lawns, on the small barns and garages tucked behind backyard shrubbery, and on the hulls of old sailboats that will never again put to sea. The sidewalk slates are rippled by the massive roots below. Two elderly ladies, straight and thin, walk by with their market bags. There are few children. There is little noise. You sense that whatever these neighborhoods are now, the best in them has gone before.

Out along the periphery of the old village, up on what were farmlands five years ago, out along the land necks reaching toward the bay, down in the cove valleys, and up among the woody ridges, range the dwellings of suburbia. Here among the asbestos shingle or "hand-split shakes," the plastic and stainless steel, the thermopane and picture window, the two-car garages and pint-sized dining areas, the weathered wagon wheel and ersatz strawberry barrel, live the suburbanites in their multi-level reconstructions of Colonial America. It is impossible to avoid them. The signs strung along the highways point the way. "Butternut Hill—Turn Right." "This Way to Strawberry Farm Homes." This is no proletarian Levittown. "Peppermill Village" starts with a "minimum" house of "just" seven rooms and two baths for $22,500 and goes on up. But the architectural themes of all of the developments are the same—antiquity, early American, "good taste." The Limited Dream finds a concretized expression of the past's myth in "Authentic Farmhouse Reconstructions" and the "Modernized New England Village."

Where the villagers live in comparative quiet against the steady but increasing hum of Main Street, the suburbanites live in sun and din. The Suburban Sound is a blend of children, dogs, doors, machines, and mothers. The bedlam of children at play is a universal sound, but the constant clatter of small machines and the ever-present yapping of frustrated dogs are uniquely suburban. In the summer months, the machines of suburbia are particularly vocal—the power lawn mowers (the grunt, click, and chug of the reel type serving as bass for the steady, high-powered whine of the rotary), the exhaust fans, the concrete mixers, the post-hole diggers, the tree cutters, the roto-tillers, the flooded-cellar pumpers, the hedge trimmers, and softly, in the distance, the growl and clink of the bulldozer steadily at work making more suburbs. Add to this the shouts of children, the cries of babies, the calls of mothers, and the muted tones of the dual tail pipes on the station wagon headed into the village, and the Suburban Sound is complete.

No longer is there enough space in Old Harbor. You can't park your car on Main Street any more, there may not be room in church if you arrive late on Sunday, classrooms are "overcrowded," and you have to wait your turn for telephones to be installed in your new house. But these are simply the unsurprising results of sudden growth, and the Old Harborites are on their way to solving many of them. They have built schools and plan more. They are tearing down bits of the old village surrounding Main Street and are putting in parking lots. Some churches are adding wings or erecting entirely new buildings. They have added policemen and fire engines, and have widened the critical streets. The physical problems, in general, are understood and are being coped with realistically.

The fundamental schism between the world of the old-timers and the world of the newcomers makes a problem that is less obvious but both more important and harder to cope with.

In their occupational characteristics, the old settlers range between the middle and upper-middle class. The majority are employed in Old Harbor as merchants, small manufacturers, and businessmen. They constitute the current rearguard of the entrepreneurs of the last century. The rest are mostly white-collar people of various persuasions who are employed either in Old Harbor or the neighboring, highly suburbanized county. Less than 20 per cent commute into the central city.

The average villager is middle-aged, married, and probably has two children either finishing high school or going to college. As a group the old-timer's formal education did not go beyond high school, but they want their children to go to college and they will generally pick one of the better ones. About half of the old-timers are Protestant, a third are Catholic, and seven percent are Jewish. The Catholic and Jewish populations represent the changes in Old Harbor's ethnic or religious character that began at the turn of the century. The median family income for the old-timers in 1955 was about $6,700, roughly $2,300 over the national median for that year. Obviously not all old-timers in Old Harbor are high-school educated, regular church attendants and securely anchored in the white-collar occupations, but enough are to justify the image of the old-timer as localistic, Protestant, economically "comfortable," conservative, and middle-class.

Some of the villagers trace their family lines back ten or twelve generations. Even those who arrived only fifteen or twenty years ago have spent enough time in Old Harbor to have become personally and deeply involved in the community. For them Old Harbor has become a "way of life" and an object of deep affection. When the old-timer thinks of himself, of his identity as a person, he also thinks of Old Harbor. The community, the social system, the institutions, the organizations, the friendships have become a part of his character. Whatever is the fate of the village has also become each old-timer's personal fate. An old-timer merchant put the matter this way: "I have traveled a lot in this country and I've been to Europe a couple of times too. But the biggest thrill in my life was when I got back from Europe and drove over Potter's Hill and saw the spire of Old First Church down in the valley. It was the most beautiful sight in the world. I really love this town—Old Harbor is the finest community in the United States."

The suburbanites are another story. They are a high-income group ($9,700 a year) of professional men and executives. Ninety-seven percent arrived in Old Harbor married and almost 94 percent bought houses there. They average about two grade-school children per family. Only a fourth are Roman Catholics; the great majority are Protestants, although a few more Jews have entered the community in recent years. Nearly four out of every ten of the newcomers were born outside the state. Two-thirds have been exposed to a college education. Close to half commute to the central city, and another third are employed in the county adjacent to the city.

Though the villagers are economically "comfortable," they are nonetheless rather stationary on the income ladder. They are pretty well frozen into an occupational cul-de-sac. The suburbanites, on the other hand, are upward bound—their jobs pay better and carry more prestige than the villagers'. For them the primary world is the metropolitan area. They work there, play there, and their most intimate friends live there. They tend to see in Old Harbor the familiar culture of the apartment house now spread into one-acre "country estates." To the villager, Old Harbor represents continuity between the generations, stability instead of the city's "chaos," and a place of permanence in a universe of bewildering change. The suburbanite sees in the village a weekend away from the advertising agency or the pilot's compartment. He experiences Old Harbor as a series of isolated, fragmented, unconnected social situations. Old Harbor is the family, a cocktail party, a bathing beach, a movie, a supermarket, a country club, a school, a church, a PTA meeting. It is a one-acre wooded retreat from all of the drive, bureaucracy, and anxiety of the city. But a weekend is enough for the necessary physical and psychological repairs; it's back to the city on Monday.

The temper of the suburbanite "community" may be summarized in the way the suburbanites talk about Old Harbor:

> I came to Old Harbor because there is still some green around here and yet I can still get to the airport in 45 minutes. It's a nice place to live—the schools are good, and I like being near the water. It is hard to say how long we'll be here. I would like to be based further south, but as a place to live Old Harbor is fine.

> I can't think of Old Harbor as my own town or anything like that. Most of my friends live closer to the city and I work there. I don't have any feeling of living in a small community or anything like that. I guess I sleep more of my time here than anything else, but it's a good place for the kids. I've got a lot of contacts and interests outside.

> I have to go pretty much where the company sends me. I was transferred up to the office over a year ago so we bought a place out here in Old Harbor. Probably be here for three or four years, then most likely I'll be sent to South America. We like Old Harbor although the way it's building up it will be like the city in no time. Well, it doesn't bother me much; we won't be around here forever.

But an old-timer says:

> They [the suburbanites] don't know what's going on around here. They don't care. But I do; this is my town. I used to fish down at the tide basin. Now they're talking of tearing it down. I went to school here. All my friends live around here. It's crazy what's happening. I can look out of my shop window and can't recognize 49 out of 50 faces I see. There was a time I knew everybody. It used to be our town. I don't know whose it is any more.

For the villagers, Old Harbor is their community and they have a fierce sense of possession about it. It is a property that they share. And like any valuable property it is cared for and cherished. It must not be profanely or rudely used. This is the real issue that splits the suburbanite and villager communities apart. For the suburbanites, Old Harbor is another commodity; it is a product that can be rationally consumed; it is a means by which they hope to achieve a complex series of personal goals. For the villagers, on the other hand, Old Harbor is not a means to anything; it is simply an end in itself.

The two communities inevitably brush against each other in the course of everyday life. They flow together on the central streets, in the movie houses, on the beaches, at graduation exercises, and in the stores and shops of Main Street. In their economic relationships, villager and suburbanite have struck a symbiotic truce. They need each other, the villager to sell and the suburbanite to buy. Suburbia has brought new prosperity to the villager. Traffic and congestion on Main Street mean crowds of buyers. Parking lots may be expensive, but they also mean customers. On the other hand, there are signs that increasing suburbanization will threaten the retailers of Main Street. The shiny "super shopping centers" to the south of the village, where a couple of thousand cars can park with ease, make the village shops seem dingy and dull. The discount stores and mechanized supermarkets of the shopping centers out along the highway augur a bleaker future along Main Street.

Perhaps the greatest single issue separating villager from suburbanite has been "the school problem." With the tripling of the school population, Old Harbor has been faced with an intensive building program. Since they are essentially realists in their village microcosm, the old-timers have reluctantly admitted the "need" for more schools. Enough of them have been eventually worn down in public meetings to cast an approving vote for new construction. For many a villager, however, it has seemed to mean money out of his pocket to pay for the schooling of other people's children. But the basic and decisive issue has not been whether to build more schools or not, but what kind of schools to build and what kind of education the children should have.

In their approach to this question, the villagers are traditionalists and conservative. They see a good education as including the basic skills taught by a dedicated but maidenly teacher in a plain school building. The suburbanites, on the other hand, are educational radicals; they are irrepressible spenders and cultlike in their dedication to the cause of modern education. It is an axiom among the old-timers that the more costly a pending proposition is the more the newcomers will take to it, and they are not entirely wrong. The newcomers appear willing to sacrifice all else to their "children's education." At PTA gatherings and public meetings of the school board, an ecstatic speaker can bring tears to sophisticated suburbanite eyes and justify the most outlandish cause by reminding his audience that "no expense is too great when it comes to our children's welfare. It will just cost the price of a few cartons of cigarettes a year to give our children this new gymnasium. Isn't our children's education, and clean, wholesome recreational facilities worth a few cents more a year? Is there any parent here who can deny their children this? Is there anyone here who will deny their children what America can offer . . . ?"

Everyone will be on his feet applauding, for the side of "the children" has won again, and every villager who voted against the plastic gymnasium or marble swimming pool will have to face the terrible question: "Do I really hate children?"

For the newcomers, anything that is educationally worth while must also be very expensive. "After all, you get what you pay for." The villagers, on the other hand, will battle the "frills" and "extravagances" and will turn down "excessive" curricular and building proposals. Eventually a compromise is worked out. But in the suburbias of the upper-middle class, education is the cohesive issue around which a "consciousness of kind" develops for the newcomers. For many, education seems to have taken the place of religion.

While the newcomers have taken over the PTA's and infiltrated the school board, the villagers continue to control the churches. Suburbanites usually join the PTA before they become members of a church, though they swell the numbers of those attending religious services. But even in the ranks of the devout, there have been indications of a schism.

The villagers tend to look upon their churches as something more than formal religious centers. Over the years they have served as rallying points for a good deal of coöperative community activity, and they tend to stand for a morality and a traditionalism highly compatible with villager perspectives. One villager remarked that you can hardly keep from feeling a little possessive about a church you have helped to build. The minister of one Protestant church who rather reluctantly admitted that all was not harmony within his flock, pointed out that the "older residents" had finished paying off the church mortgage sometime around 1947, and a few years later the church had almost doubled its congregation. As the minister saw it, the villagers were indignant over the invasion of "their" church by "outsiders." They were especially smarting over the fact that, because of the devoted work of the old-timers, the newcomers had inherited a church free and clear of any financial encumbrance. The villagers felt that the solvency of their church had made it more attractive, and that the enthusiasm the suburbanites showed for it was not without crasser implications. As a consequence, the old-timers began to champion all church causes that were particularly expensive. It has been the villagers who have stoutly called for a new Sunday School building and a finer parish house. The villagers have been on the side of free-and-easy spending by the church ever since the suburban influx began.

This is not the whole story. A few years back, one of the most fashionable churches of Old Harbor made some sympathetic overtures to a purely newcomer religious group—Jews of the "Reformed" group who were conducting their services in an empty store on Main Street. The minister of this old Protestant church, which traces its origins back to the American Revolution and whose membership consists of the elect of Old Harbor society, offered the facilities of his church to the Jewish newcomers. The Jews happily accepted the offer. This not only brought the two worlds together but the Protestant and localistic villagers and the Jewish, cosmopolitan suburbanites even sponsored joint "functions" together. The differences between the villagers and suburbanites are not insurmountable, nor are the two separated by an impenetrable curtain of prejudice and ignorance.

The newcomers have largely ignored the formal political organizations of Old Harbor. Traditionally the community has been solidly Republican, and the upper-middle-class suburbanites have not threatened the political balance. There are a few more egghead Democrats in Old Harbor in recent years who write books or teach in a college, but they are regarded as odd and harmless, and no one pays much attention to them. This does not mean that the suburbanites are not politically active; they are, but they act outside political parties to do political things. Their means is the civic association. Each development or combination of developments has organized its own. As the Peppermill Village Civic Association, they lobby for sidewalks or against sidewalks, for street lights and sewers, or to keep out the sand and gravel contractor who wants to use the adjacent property for commercial purposes. Through the civic associations, the suburbanites engage in a series of running skirmishes with the villagers over local issues. Usually what they want costs more, so the villagers are against it.

The old-timers fill almost all the political offices, where they serve to balance the limited and self-interested objectives of the civic associations against the "broader needs" of the village and the township. But in this capacity the old-timers are more than old-timers; they are also politicians. Having learned that the suburbanites are amazingly perceptive on the level of neighborhood self-interest, the politicians will throw an occasional sop to the militant civic associations with an eye to the coming elections. Though the suburbanites are circumscribed in their interests, they are nonetheless organized, and can marshal massive political displeasure at the polls. As a consequence, the villager politicians must somehow walk a tightrope, balancing the political expediency of pleasing the newcomers against their own desire to keep the village what it was.

One wonders how many towns like Old Harbor are currently fighting to keep their identities in the industrializing South or in the rapidly growing Far West. How many Old Harbors are there all together? No one can even chance a guess. Each of the 168 great metropolitan centers of the nation is at present consuming a whole series of villages now within its sociological borders. And each village has a different history, a geography of its own and a set of institutions practiced by a population that is the same as nowhere else. Yet beneath the idiosyncratic surface, the villagers look with universal anxiety as the crush of metropolitanization proceeds. Everywhere the spirit of the small village suffers with the encroachment of urban anonymity and transiency. The Levittowns are fresh and naked, yet of a single character. The Old Harbors are split by the struggles of two communities to shape the prevailing character of the whole.

Yet the future lies with the metropolis and not the village. You can see it in the new super expressways that slice through Old Harbor's meadowlands. You sense the shift in internal balance in the village by the domination of the suburbanites at school board meetings. You know it on an autumn's evening, in the crisp sea air, and in the deepening twilight around the mill pond. The great shuddering bulk of the mill squats in the hollow, intimidated by the headlights of the commuters as they race down and through the valley, dreary from the city and hungry for home. Pencils of light search into the gaping slats and crudely intrude upon the embarrassment of the mill's decay—the rusting gears, the splintered shaft, the rotting timbers, and marsh slop heaped up by the last high tide. And then with a rush the auto is gone, driving a little eddy of defiant leaves against the listless doors, leaving the old mill momentarily in shadows, huddled against the lowering sky. Through the empty windows, across the tide basin, and over the harbor, you can see the new shopping center bathed in neon and fluorescent light. There is a busyness about it. Up along the darkening necks the lights are going on in the new split levels and "contemporaries" tucked into the ridges. The lights go on and off as the night rolls in. They seem to be winking at the senile mill as it sits and broods in the gathering darkness.

Community on the City Streets

JANE JACOBS

In this selection, the author takes the reader into the supposedly most heartless areas of metropolitan America, and dramatically shows how and why a sense of community, neighborliness, and a host of potential Good Samaritans are characteristic of some neighborhoods and not of others. With a keen eye for what makes for community, she challenges many of the overly rational textbook theories on city planning and urban redevelopment. In many ways, Mrs. Jacobs has an artist's, rather than a scientist's, approach to an understanding of human relationships. Even on manifestly anonymous and impersonal city streets, she is able to see the human order behind seeming chaos. It is an order, she writes toward the end of this selection, "all composed of movement and change, and although it is life, not art, we may fancifully call it the art form of the city and liken it to the dance. . . ."

Paradoxically enough to some, it is the neighborhoods that have grown up over the years—like Topsy, as it were—rather than those which have been planned in a rational and orderly way, which seem the safest and most humane. Are we then to conclude that human society and humane social relationships must be cultivated and nourished, like a delicate flower, rather than rationally built from a blueprint, like the internal-combustion engine or the giant apartment building?

REFORMERS HAVE LONG OBSERVED CITY PEOPLE LOITERING ON BUSY corners, hanging around in candy stores and bars and drinking soda pop on stoops, and have passed a judgment, the gist of which is: "This is deplorable! If these people had decent homes and a more private or bosky outdoor place, they wouldn't be on the street!"

Condensed from Jane Jacobs, *The Death and Life of Great American Cities* (New York, 1961), Copyright © 1961 by Jane Jacobs. Reprinted by permission of the author and Random House, Inc.

This judgment represents a profound misunderstanding of cities. It makes no more sense than to drop in at a testimonial banquet in a hotel and conclude that if these people had wives who could cook, they would give their parties at home.

It may be that we have become so feckless as a people that we no longer care how things do work, but only what kind of quick, easy outer impression they give. If so, there is little hope for our cities or probably for much else in our society. But I do not think this is so.

Specifically, in the case of planning for cities, it is clear that a large number of good and earnest people do care deeply about building and renewing. Despite some corruption, and considerable greed for the other man's vineyard, the intentions going into the messes we make are, on the whole, exemplary. Planners, architects of city design, and those they have led along with them in their beliefs are not consciously disdainful of the importance of knowing how things work. On the contrary, they have gone to great pains to learn what the saints and sages of modern orthodox planning have said about how cities *ought* to work and what *ought* to be good for people and businesses in them. They take this with such devotion that when contradictory reality intrudes, threatening to shatter their dearly won learning, they must shrug reality aside.

Consider, for example, the orthodox planning reaction to a district called the North End in Boston. This is an old, low-rent area merging into the heavy industry of the waterfront, and it is officially considered Boston's worst slum and civic shame. It embodies attributes which all enlightened people know are evil because so many wise men have said they are evil. Not only is the North End bumped right up against industry, but worse still it has all kinds of working places and commerce mingled in the greatest complexity with its residences. It has the highest concentration of dwelling units, on the land that is used for dwelling units, of any part of Boston, and indeed one of the highest concentrations to be found in any American city. It has little parkland. Children play in the streets. Instead of super-blocks, or even decently large blocks, it has very small blocks; in planning parlance it is "badly cut up with wasteful streets." Its buildings are old. Everything conceivable is presumably wrong with the North End. In orthodox planning terms, it is a three-dimensional textbook of "megalopolis" in the last stages of depravity. The North End is thus a recurring assignment for M.I.T. and Harvard planning and architectural students, who now and again pursue, under the guidance of their teachers, the paper exercise of converting it into super-blocks and park promenades, wiping away its nonconforming uses, transforming it to an ideal of order and gentility so simple it could be engraved on the head of a pin.

Twenty years ago, when I first happened to see the North End, its buildings—town houses of different kinds and sizes converted to flats, and four- or five-story tenements built to house the flood of immigrants first from Ireland, then from Eastern Europe and finally from Sicily—were badly overcrowded, and the general effect was of a district taking a terrible physical beating and certainly desperately poor.

When I saw the North End again in 1959, I was amazed at the change. Dozens and dozens of buildings had been rehabilitated. Instead of mattresses against the windows there were Venetian blinds and glimpses of fresh paint. Many of the small, converted houses now had only one or two families in them instead of the old crowded three or four. Some of the families in the tenements (as I learned later, visiting inside) had uncrowded themselves by throwing two older apartments together, and had equipped these with bathrooms, new kitchens and the like. I looked down a narrow alley, thinking to find at least here the old, squalid North End, but no: more neatly repointed brickwork, new blinds, and a burst of music as a door opened. Indeed, this was the only city district I had ever seen—or have seen to this day—in which the sides of buildings around parking lots had not been left raw and amputated, but repaired and painted as neatly as if they were intended to be seen. Mingled all among the buildings for living were an incredible number of splendid food stores, as well as such enterprises as upholstery making, metal working, carpentry, food processing. The streets were alive with children playing, people shopping, people strolling, people talking. Had it not been a cold January day, there would surely have been people sitting.

The general street atmosphere of buoyancy, friendliness and good health was so infectious that I began asking directions of people just for the fun of getting in on some talk. I had seen a lot of Boston in the past couple of days, most of it sorely distressing, and this struck me, with relief, as the healthiest place in the city. But I could not imagine where the money had come from for the rehabilitation, because it is almost impossible today to get any appreciable mortgage money in districts of American cities that are not either high-rent, or else imitations of suburbs. To find out, I went into a bar and restaurant (where an animated conversation about fishing was in progress) and called a Boston planner I know.

"Why in the world are you down in the North End?" he said. "Money? Why, no money or work has gone into the North End. Nothing's going on down there. Eventually, yes, but not yet. That's a slum!"

"It doesn't seem like a slum to me," I said.

"Why, that's the worst slum in the city. It has two hundred and seventy-five dwelling units to the net acre! I hate to admit we have anything like that in Boston, but it's a fact."

"Do you have any other figures on it?" I asked.

"Yes, funny thing. It has among the lowest delinquency, disease and infant mortality rates in the city. It also has the lowest ratio of rent to income in the city. Boy, are those people getting bargains. Let's see . . . the child population is just about average for the city, on the nose. The death rate is low, 8.8 per thousand, against the average city rate of 11.2. The TB death rate is very low, less than 1 per ten thousand, can't understand it, it's lower even than Brookline's. In the old days the North End used to be the city's worst spot for tuberculosis, but all that has changed. Well, they must be strong people. Of course it's a terrible slum."

"You should have more slums like this," I said. "Don't tell me there are plans to wipe this out. You ought to be down here learning as much as you can from it."

"I know how you feel," he said. "I often go down there myself just to walk around the streets and feel that wonderful, cheerful street life. Say, what you ought to do, you ought to come back and go down in the summer if you think it's fun now. You'd be crazy about it in summer. But of course we have to rebuild it eventually. We've got to get those people off the streets."

Here was a curious thing. My friend's instincts told him the North End was a good place, and his social statistics confirmed it. But everything he had learned as a physical planner about what is good for people and good for city neighborhoods, everything that made him an expert, told him the North End had to be a bad place.

The leading Boston savings banker, "a man 'way up there in the power structure," to whom my friend referred me for my inquiry about the money, confirmed what I learned, in the meantime, from people in the North End. The money had not come through the grace of the great American banking system, which now knows enough about planning to know a slum as well as the planners do. "No sense in lending money into the North End," the banker said. "It's a slum! It's still getting some immigrants! Furthermore, back in the Depression it had a very large number of foreclosures; bad record." (I had heard about this too, in the meantime, and how families had worked and pooled their resources to buy back some of those foreclosed buildings.)

The largest mortgage loans that had been fed into this district of some 15,000 people in the quarter-century since the Great Depression were for $3,000, the banker told me, "and very, very few of those." There had been some others for $1,000 and for $2,000. The rehabilitation work had been almost entirely financed by business and housing earnings within the district, plowed back in, and by skilled work bartered among residents and relatives of residents.

By this time I knew that this inability to borrow for improvement was a galling worry to North Enders, and that furthermore some North Enders were worried because it seemed impossible to get new building in the area except at the price of seeing themselves and their community wiped out in the fashion of the students' dreams of a city Eden, a fate which they knew was not academic because it had already smashed completely a socially similar—although physically more spacious—nearby district called the West End. They were worried because they were aware also that patch and fix with nothing else could not do forever. "Any chance of loans for new construction in the North End?" I asked the banker.

"No, absolutely not!" he said, sounding impatient at my denseness. "That's a slum!"

Bankers, like planners, have theories about cities on which they act. They have gotten their theories from the same intellectual sources as the planners. Bankers and government administrative officials who guarantee mortgages do not invent planning theories nor, surprisingly, even economic doctrine about cities. They are enlightened nowadays, and they pick up their ideas from idealists, a generation late. Since theoretical city planning has embraced no major new ideas for considerably more than a generation, theoretical planners, financers and bureaucrats are all just about even today. But perhaps the way to get at what goes on in the seemingly mysterious and perverse behavior of cities is, I think, to look closely, and with as little previous expectation as is possible, at the most ordinary scenes and events, and attempt to see what they mean and whether any threads of principle emerge among them. This is what I try to do.

Think of a city and what comes to mind? Its streets. If a city's streets look interesting, the city looks interesting; if they look dull, the city looks dull.

More than that, and here we get down to the first problem, if a city's streets are safe from barbarism and fear, the city is thereby tolerably safe from barbarism and fear. When people say that a city, or a part of it, is dangerous or is a jungle what they mean primarily is that they do not feel safe on the sidewalks.

The first thing to understand is that the public peace—the sidewalk and street peace—of cities is not kept primarily by the police, necessary as police are. It is kept primarily by an intricate, almost unconscious, network of voluntary controls and standards among the people themselves, and enforced by the people themselves. In some city areas—older public housing projects and streets with very high population turnover are often conspicuous examples—the keeping of public sidewalk law and order is left almost entirely to the police and special guards. Such places are jungles. No amount of police can enforce civilization where the normal, casual enforcement of it has broken down.

The second thing to understand is that the problem of insecurity cannot be solved by spreading people out more thinly, trading the characteristics of cities for the characteristics of suburbs. If this could solve danger on the city streets, then Los Angeles should be a safe city because superficially Los Angeles is almost all suburban. It has virtually no districts compact enough to qualify as dense city areas. Yet Los Angeles cannot, any more than any other great city, evade the truth that, being a city, it *is* composed of strangers not all of whom are nice. Los Angeles' crime figures are flabbergasting. Among the seventeen standard metropolitan areas with populations over a million, Los Angeles stands so preeminent in crime that it is in a category by itself. And this is markedly true of crimes associated with personal attack, the crimes that make people fear the streets.

Los Angeles, for example, has a forcible rape rate (1958 figures) of 31.9 per 100,000 population, more than twice as high as either of the next two cities, which happen to be St. Louis and Philadelphia; three times as high as the rate of 10.1 for Chicago, and more than four times as high as the rate of 7.4 for New York.

In aggravated assault, Los Angeles has a rate of 185, compared with 149.5 for Baltimore and 139.2 for St. Louis (the two next highest), and with 90.9 for New York and 79 for Chicago.

The overall Los Angeles rate for major crimes is 2,507.6 per 100,000 people, far ahead of St. Louis and Houston, which come next with 1,634.5 and 1,541.1, and of New York and Chicago, which have rates of 1,145.3 and 943.5.

The reasons for Los Angeles' high crime rates are undoubtedly complex, and at least in part obscure. But of this we can be sure: thinning out a city does not insure safety from crime and fear of crime. This is one of the conclusions that can be drawn within individual cities too, where pseudosuburbs or superannuated suburbs are ideally suited to rape, muggings, beatings, holdups and the like.

Here we come up against an all-important question about any city street: How much easy opportunity does it offer to crime? It may be that there is some absolute amount of crime in a given city, which will find an outlet somehow (I do not believe this). Whether this is so or not, different kinds of city streets garner radically different shares of barbarism and fear of barbarism.

Some city streets afford no opportunity to street barbarism. The streets of the North End of Boston are outstanding examples. They are probably as safe as any place on earth in this respect. Although most of the North End's residents are Italian or of Italian descent, the district's streets are also heavily and constantly used by people of every race and background. Some of the strangers from outside work in or close to the district; some come to shop and stroll; many, including members of minority groups who have inherited dangerous districts previously abandoned by others, make a point of cashing their paychecks in North End stores and immediately making their big weekly purchases in streets where they know they will not be parted from their money between the getting and the spending.

Frank Havey, director of the North End Union, the local settlement house, says, "I have been here in the North End twenty-eight years, and in all that time I have never heard of a single case of rape, mugging, molestation of a child or other street crime of that sort in the district. And if there had been any, I would have heard of it even if it did not reach the papers." Half a dozen times or so in the past three decades, says Havey, would-be molesters have made an attempt at luring a child or, late at night, attacking a woman. In every such case the try was thwarted by passers-by, by kibitzers from windows, or shopkeepers.

Meantime, in the Elm Hill Avenue section of Roxbury, a part of inner Boston that is suburban in superficial character, street assaults and the ever-present possibility of more street assaults with no kibitzers to protect the victims, induce prudent people to stay off the sidewalks at night. Not surprisingly, for this and other reasons that are related (dispiritedness and dullness), most of Roxbury has run down. It has become a place to leave.

I do not wish to single out Roxbury or its once fine Elm Hill Avenue section especially as a vulnerable area; its disabilities, and especially its Great Blight of Dullness, are all too common in other cities too. But differences like these in public safety within the same city are worth noting. The Elm Hill Avenue section's basic troubles are not owing to a criminal or a discriminated against or a poverty-stricken population. Its troubles stem from the fact that it is physically quite unable to function safely and with related vitality as a city district.

Even within supposedly similar parts of supposedly similar places, drastic differences in public safety exist. An incident at Washington Houses, a public housing project in New York, illustrates this point. A tenants' group at this project, struggling to establish itself, held some outdoor ceremonies in mid-December 1958, and put up three Christmas trees. The chief tree, so cumbersome it was a problem to transport, erect, and trim, went into the project's inner "street," a landscaped central mall and promenade. The other two trees, each less than six feet tall and easy to carry, went on two small fringe plots at the outer corners of the project where it abuts a busy avenue and lively cross streets of the old city. The first night, the large tree and all its trimmings were stolen. The two smaller trees remained intact, lights, ornaments and all, until they were taken down at New Year's. "The place where the tree was stolen, which is *theoretically* the most safe and sheltered place in the project, is the same place that is unsafe for people too, especially children," says a social worker who had been helping the tenants' group. "People are no safer in that mall than the Christmas tree. On the other hand, the place where the other trees were safe, where the project is just one corner out of four, happens to be safe for people."

It is futile to try to evade the issue of unsafe city streets by attempting to make some other features of a locality, say interior courtyards, or sheltered play spaces, safe instead. By definition again, the streets of a city must do most of the job of handling strangers for this is where strangers come and go. The streets must not only defend the city against predatory strangers, they must protect the many, many peaceable and well-meaning strangers who use them, insuring their safety too as they pass through. Moreover, no normal person can spend his life in some artificial haven, and this includes children. Everyone must use the streets.

A lively street always has both its users and pure watchers. Last year I was on such a street in the Lower East Side of Manhattan, waiting for a bus. I had not been there longer than a minute, barely long enough to begin taking in the street's activity of errand-goers, children playing, and loiterers on the stoops, when my attention was attracted by a woman who opened a window on the third floor of a tenement across the street and vigorously youhooed at me. When I caught on that she wanted my attention and responded, she shouted down, "The bus doesn't run here on Saturdays!" Then by a combination of shouts and pantomime she directed me around the corner. This woman was one of thousands upon thousands of people in New York who casually take care of the streets. They notice strangers. They observe everything going on. If they need to take action, whether to direct a stranger waiting in the wrong place or to call the police, they do so. Action usually requires, to be sure, a certain self-assurance about the actor's proprietorship of the street and the support he will get if necessary, matters which will be gone into later in this book. But even more fundamental than the action and necessary to the action, is the watching itself.

Not everyone in cities helps to take care of the streets, and many a city resident or city worker is unaware of why his neighborhood is safe.

The other day an incident occurred on the street where I live, and it interested me because of this point.

My block of the street, I must explain, is a small one, but it contains a remarkable range of buildings, varying from several vintages of tenements to three- and four-story houses that have been converted into low-rent flats with stores on the ground floor, or returned to single-family use like ours. Across the street there used to be mostly four-story brick tenements with stores below. But twelve years ago several buildings, from the corner to the middle of the block, were converted into one building with elevator apartments of small size and high rents.

The incident that attracted my attention was a suppressed struggle going on between a man and a little girl of eight or nine years old. The man seemed to be trying to get the girl to go with him. By turns he was directing a cajoling attention to her, and then assuming an air of nonchalance. The girl was making herself rigid, as children do when they resist, against the wall of one of the tenements across the street.

As I watched from our second-floor window, making up my mind how to intervene if it seemed advisable, I saw it was not going to be necessary. From the butcher shop beneath the tenement had emerged the woman who, with her husband, runs the shop; she was standing within earshot of the man, her arms folded and a look of determination on her face. Joe Cornacchia, who with his sons-in-law keeps the delicatessen, emerged about the same moment and stood solidly to the other side. Several heads poked out of the tenement windows above, one was withdrawn quickly and its owner reappeared a moment later in the doorway behind the man. Two men from the bar next to the butcher shop came to the doorway and waited. On my side of the street, I saw that the locksmith, the fruit man and the laundry proprietor had all come out of their shops and that the scene was also being surveyed from a number of windows besides ours. That man did not know it, but he was surrounded. Nobody was going to allow a little girl to be dragged off, even if nobody knew who she was.

I am sorry—sorry purely for dramatic purposes—to have to report that the little girl turned out to be the man's daughter.

Throughout the duration of the little drama, perhaps five minutes in all, no eyes appeared in the windows of the high-rent, small-apartment building. It was the only building of which this was true. When we first moved to our block, I used to anticipate happily that perhaps soon all the buildings would be rehabilitated like that one. I know better now, and can only anticipate with gloom and foreboding the recent news that exactly this transformation is scheduled for the rest of the block frontage adjoining the high-rent building. The high-rent tenants, most of whom are so transient we cannot even keep track of their faces,[1] have not the remotest idea of who takes care of their street, or how. A city neighborhood can absorb and protect a substantial number of these birds of passage, as our neighborhood does. But if and when the neighborhood finally *becomes* them, they will gradually find the streets less secure, they will be vaguely mystified about it, and if things get bad enough they will drift away to another neighborhood which is mysteriously safer.

In some rich city neighborhoods, where there is little do-it-yourself surveillance, such as residential Park Avenue or upper Fifth Avenue in New York, street watchers are hired. The monotonous sidewalks of residential Park Avenue, for example, are surprisingly little used; their putative users are populating, instead, the interesting store-, bar- and restaurant-filled sidewalks of Lexington Avenue and Madison Avenue to east and west, and the cross streets leading to these. A network of doormen and superintendents, of delivery boys and nursemaids, a form of hired neighborhood, keeps residential Park Avenue supplied with eyes. At night, with the security of the doormen as a bulwark, dog walkers safely venture forth and supplement the doormen. But this street is so blank of built-in eyes, so devoid of concrete reasons for using or watching it instead of turning the first corner off of it, that if its rents were to slip below the point where they could support a plentiful hired neighborhood of doormen and elevator men, it would undoubtedly become a woefully dangerous street.

This sad circumstance is especially true in the dispirited gray belts of great cities and in once fashionable or at least once solid inner residential areas gone into decline. Because these neighborhoods are so dangerous, and the streets typically so dark, it is commonly believed that their trouble may be insufficient street lighting. Good lighting is important, but darkness alone does not account for the gray areas' deep, functional sickness, the Great Blight of Dullness.

The value of bright street lights for dispirited gray areas rises from the reassurance they offer to some people who need to go out on the sidewalk, or would like to, but lacking the good light would not do so. Thus the lights induce these people to contribute their own eyes to the upkeep of the street. Moreover, as is obvious, good lighting augments every pair of eyes, makes the eyes count for more because their range is greater. Each additional pair of eyes, and every increase in their range, is that much to the good for dull gray areas. But unless eyes are there, and unless in the brains behind those eyes is the almost unconscious reassurance of general street support in upholding civilization, lights can do no

[1] Some, according to the storekeepers, live on beans and bread and spend their sojourn looking for a place to live where all their money will not go for rent.

good. Horrifying public crimes can, and do, occur in well-lighted subway stations when no effective eyes are present. They virtually never occur in darkened theaters where many people and eyes are present. Street lights can be like that famous stone that falls in the desert where there are no ears to hear. Does it make a noise? Without effective eyes to see, does a light cast light? Not for practical purposes.

To explain the troubling effect of strangers on the streets of city gray areas, I shall first point out, for purposes of analogy, the peculiarities of another and figurative kind of street—the corridors of high-rise public housing projects, those derivatives of Radiant City. The elevators and corridors of these projects are, in a sense, streets. They are streets piled up in the sky in order to eliminate streets on the ground and permit the ground to become deserted parks like the mall at Washington Houses where the tree was stolen.

Not only are these interior parts of the buildings streets in the sense that they serve the comings and goings of residents, most of whom may not know each other or recognize, necessarily, who is a resident and who is not. They are streets also in the sense of being accessible to the public. They have been designed in an imitation of upper-class standards for apartment living without upper-class cash for doormen and elevator men. Anyone at all can go into these buildings, unquestioned, and use the traveling street of the elevator and the sidewalks that are the corridors. These interior streets, although completely accessible to public use, are closed to public view and they thus lack the checks and inhibitions exerted by eye-policed city streets.

Troubled, so far as I can determine, less by the amply proved dangers to human beings in these blind-eyed streets than by the vandalism to property that occurs in them, the New York City Housing Authority some years back experimented with corridors open to public view in a Brooklyn project which I shall call Blenheim Houses although that is not its name. (I do not wish to add to its troubles by advertising it.)

Because the buildings of Blenheim Houses are sixteen stories high, and because their height permits generous expanses of shunned ground area, surveillance of the open corridors from the ground or from other buildings offers little more than psychological effect, but this psychological openness to view does appear effective to some degree. More important and effective, the corridors were well designed to induce surveillance from within the buildings themselves. Uses other than plain circulation were built into them. They were equipped as play space, and made sufficiently generous to act as narrow porches, as well as passageways. This all turned out to be so lively and interesting that the tenants added still another use and much the favorite: picnic grounds—this in spite of continual pleas and threats from the management which did not *plan* that the balcony-corridors should serve as picnic grounds. (The plan should anticipate everything and then permit no changes.) The tenants are devoted to the balcony-corridors; and as a result of being intensively used the balconies are under intense surveillance. There has been no problem of crime in these particular corridors, nor of vandalism either. Not even light bulbs are stolen or broken, although in projects of similar size with blind-eyed corridors, light bulb replacements solely because of theft or vandalism customarily run into the thousands each month.

So far so good.

A striking demonstration of the direct connection between city surveillance and city safety!

Nonetheless, Blenheim Houses has a fearsome problem of vandalism and scandalous behavior. The lighted balconies which are, as the manager puts it, "the brightest and most attractive scene in sight," draw strangers, especially teen-agers, from all over Brooklyn. But these strangers, lured by the magnet of the publicly visible corridors, do not halt at the visible corridors. They go into other "streets" of the buildings, streets that lack surveillance. These include the elevators and, more important in this case, the fire stairs and their landings. The housing police run up and down after the malefactors—who behave barbarously and viciously in the blind-eyed, sixteen-story-high stairways—and the malefactors elude them. It is easy to run the elevators up to a high floor, jam the doors so the elevators cannot be brought down, and then play hell with a building and anyone you can catch. So serious is the problem and apparently so uncontrollable, that the advantage of the safe corridors is all but canceled—at least in the harried manager's eyes.

What happens at Blenheim Houses is somewhat the same as what happens in dull gray areas of cities. The gray areas' pitifully few and thinly spaced patches of brightness and life are like the visible corridors at Blenheim Houses. They do attract strangers. But the relatively deserted, dull, blind streets leading from these places are like the fire stairs at Blenheim Houses. These are not equipped to handle strangers and the presence of strangers in them is an automatic menace.

The temptation in such cases is to blame the balconies—or the commerce or bars that serve as a magnet. A typical train of thought is exemplified in the Hyde Park–Kenwood renewal project now under way in Chicago. This piece of gray area adjoining The University of Chicago contains many splendid houses and grounds, but for thirty years it has been plagued with a frightening street crime problem, accompanied in latter years by considerable physical decay. The "cause" of Hyde Park–Kenwood's decline has been brilliantly identified, by the planning heirs of the bloodletting doctors, as the presence of "blight." By blight they mean that too many of the college professors and other middle-class families steadily deserted this dull and dangerous area and their places were often, quite naturally, taken by those with little economic or social choice among living places. The plan designates and removes these chunks of blight and replaces them with chunks of Radiant Garden City designed, as usual, to minimize use of the streets. The plan also adds still more empty spaces here and there, blurs even further the district's already poor distinctions between private and public space, and amputates the existing commerce, which is no great shakes. The early plans for this renewal included a relatively large imitation-suburban shopping center. But the thoughts of this brought a faint reminder of realities and a glimmer of apprehension in the course of the planning process. A large center, larger than that required for the standard shopping needs of residents in the renewal district itself, "might draw into the area extraneous people," as one of the architectural planners put it. A small shopping center was thereupon settled on. Large or small matters little.

It matters little because Hyde Park–Kenwood, like all city districts, is, in real life, surrounded by "extraneous" people. The area is an embedded part of Chicago. It cannot wish away its location. It cannot bring back its one-time condition, long gone, of semisuburbia. To plan as if it could, and to evade its deep, functional inadequacies, can have only one of two possible results.

Either extraneous people will continue to come into the area as they please, and if so they will include some strangers who are not at all nice. So far as security is concerned, nothing will have changed except that the opportunity for street crime will be a little easier, if anything, because of the added emptiness. Or the plan can be accompanied by determined, extraordinary means for keeping extraneous people out of this area, just as the adjoining University of Chicago, the institution that was the moving spirit in getting the plan under way, has itself taken the extraordinary measure, as reported in the press, of loosing police dogs every night to patrol its campus and hold at bay any human being in this dangerous unurban inner keep. The barriers formed by new projects at the edges of Hyde Park–Kenwood, plus extraordinary policing, may indeed keep out extraneous people with sufficient effectiveness. If so, the price will be hostility from the surrounding city and an ever more beleaguered feeling within the fort. And who can be sure, either, that all those thousands rightfully within the fort are trustworthy in the dark?

Again, I do not wish to single out one area, or in this case one plan, as uniquely opprobrious. Hyde Park–Kenwood is significant mainly because the diagnosis and the corrective measures of the plan are typical—just slightly more ambitious—of plans conceived for gray area renewal experiments in cities all over the country. This is City Planning, with all the stamp of orthodoxy on it, not some aberration of local willfulness.

Suppose we continue with building, and with deliberate rebuilding, of unsafe cities. How do we live with this insecurity? From the evidence thus far, there seem to be three modes of living with it; maybe in time others will be invented but I suspect these three will simply be further developed, if that is the word for it.

The first mode is to let danger hold sway, and let those unfortunate enough to be stuck with it take the consequences. This is the policy now followed with respect to low-income housing projects, and to many middle-income housing projects.

The second mode is to take refuge in vehicles. This is a technique practiced in the big wild-animal reservations of Africa, where tourists are warned to leave their cars under no circumstances until they reach a lodge. It is also the technique practiced in Los Angeles. Surprised visitors to that city are forever recounting how the police of Beverly Hills stopped them, made them prove their reasons for being afoot, and warned them of the danger. This technique of public safety does not seem to work too effectively yet in Los Angeles, as the crime rate shows, but in time it may. And think what the crime figures might be if more people without metal shells were helpless upon the vast, blind-eyed reservation of Los Angeles.

People in dangerous parts of other cities often use automobiles as protection too, of course, or try to. A letter to the editor in the *New York Post,* reads, "I live on a dark street off Utica Avenue in Brooklyn and therefore decided to take a cab home even though it was not late. The cab driver asked that I get off at the corner of Utica, saying he did not want to go down the dark street. If I had wanted to walk down the dark street, who needed him?"

The third mode, at which I have already hinted while discussing Hyde Park–Kenwood, was developed by hoodlum gangs and has been adopted widely by developers of the rebuilt city. This mode is to cultivate the institution of Turf.

Under the Turf system in its historical form, a gang appropriates as its territory certain streets or housing projects or parks—often a combination of the three. Members of other gangs cannot enter this Turf without permission from the Turf-owning gang, or if they do so it is at peril of being beaten or run off. In 1956, the New York City Youth Board, fairly desperate because of gang warfare, arranged through its gang youth workers a series of truces among fighting gangs. The truces were reported to stipulate, among other provisions, a mutual understanding of Turf boundaries among the gangs concerned and agreement not to trespass.

The city's police commissioner, Stephen P. Kennedy, thereupon expressed outrage at agreements respecting Turf. The police, he said, aimed to protect the right of every person to walk any part of the city in safety and with impunity as a basic right. Pacts about Turf, he indicated, were intolerably subversive both of public rights and public safety.

I think Commissioner Kennedy was profoundly right. However, we must reflect upon the problem facing the Youth Board workers. It was a real one, and they were trying as well as they could to meet it with whatever empirical means they could. The safety of the city, on which public right and freedom of movement ultimately depend, was missing from the unsuccessful streets, parks and projects dominated by these gangs. Freedom of the city, under these circumstances, was a rather academic ideal.

Now consider the redevelopment projects of cities: the middle- and upper-income housing occupying many acres of city, many former blocks, with their own grounds and their own streets to serve these "islands within the city," "cities within the city," and "new concepts in city living," as the advertisements for them say. The technique here is also to designate the Turf and fence the other gangs out. At first the fences were never visible. Patrolling guards were sufficient to enforce the line. But in the past few years the fences have become literal.

Perhaps the first was the high cyclone fence around a Radiant Garden City project adjoining Johns Hopkins Hospital in Baltimore (great educational institutions seem to be deplorably inventive with Turf devices). In case anyone mistakes what the fence means, the signs on the project street also say "Keep Out. No Trespassing." It is uncanny to see a city neighborhood, in a civilian city, walled off like this. It looks not only ugly, in a deep sense, but surrealistic. You can imagine how it sits with the neighbors, in spite of the antidote message on the project church's bulletin board: "Christ's Love Is The Best Tonic Of All."

New York has been quick to copy the lesson of Baltimore, in its own fashion. Indeed, at the back of the Amalgamated Houses on the Lower East Side, New York has gone further. At the northern end of the project's parklike central promenade, an iron-bar gate has been permanently padlocked and is crowned not with mere metal netting but with a tangle of barbed wire. And does this defended promenade give out on depraved old megalopolis? Not at all. Its neighbor is a public playground and beyond this more project housing for a different income class.

In the rebuilt city it takes a heap of fences to make a balanced neighborhood. The "juncture" between two differently price-tagged populations, again in the rebuilt Lower East Side, that between middle-income cooperative Corlears Hook and low-income Vladeck Houses, is especially elaborate. Corlears Hook buffers its Turf against its next-door neighbors with a wide parking lot running the full width of the super-block juncture, next a spindly hedge and a six-foot-high cyclone fence, next a completely fenced-in no man's land some thirty feet wide consisting mainly of dirty blowing papers and deliberately inaccessible to anything else. Then begins the Vladeck Turf.

Similarly, on the Upper West Side, the rental agent of Park West Village, "Your Own World in the Heart of New York," on whom I have foisted myself as a prospective tenant, tells me reassuringly, "Madam, as soon as the shopping center is completed, the entire grounds will be fenced in."

"Cyclone fences?"

"That is correct, madam. And eventually"—waving his hand at the city surrounding his domain—"all that will go. Those people will go. We are the pioneers here."

I suppose it is rather like pioneer life in a stockaded village, except that the pioneers were working toward greater security for their civilization, not less.

Some members of the gangs on the new Turfs find this way of life hard to take. Such was one who wrote a letter to the *New York Post* in 1959: "The other day for the first time my pride at being a resident of Stuyvesant Town and of New York City was replaced by indignation and shame. I noticed two boys about 12 years old sitting on a Stuyvesant Town bench. They were deep in conversation, quiet, well-behaved—and Puerto Rican. Suddenly two Stuyvesant Town guards were approaching—one from the north and one from the south. The one signaled the other by pointing to the two boys. One went up to the boys and after several words, quietly spoken on both sides, the boys rose and left. They tried to look unconcerned . . . How can we expect people to have any dignity and self-respect if we rip it from them even before they reach adulthood? How really poor are we of Stuyvesant Town and of New York City, too, that we can't share a bench with two boys?"

The Letters Editor gave this communication the headline, "Stay in Your Own Turf."

The technique of dividing the city into Turfs is not simply a New York solution. It is a Rebuilt American City solution. At the Harvard Design Conference of 1959, one of the topics pondered by city architectural designers turned out to be the puzzle of Turf, although they did not use that designation. The examples discussed happened to be the Lake

Meadows middle-income project of Chicago and the Lafayette Park high-income project of Detroit. Do you keep the rest of the city out of these blind-eyed purlieus? How difficult and how unpalatable. Do you invite the rest of the city in? How difficult and how impossible.

Like the Youth Board workers, the developers and residents of Radiant City and Radiant Garden City and Radiant Garden City Beautiful have a genuine difficulty and they have to do the best they can with it by the empirical means at their disposal. They have little choice. Wherever the rebuilt city rises the barbaric concept of Turf must follow, because the rebuilt city has junked a basic function of the city street and with it, necessarily, the freedom of the city.

Under the seeming disorder of the old city, wherever the old city is working successfully, is a marvelous order for maintaining the safety of the streets and the freedom of the city. It is a complex order. Its essence is intricacy of sidewalk use, bringing with it a constant succession of eyes. This order is all composed of movement and change, and although it is life, not art, we may fancifully call it the art form of the city and liken it to the dance—not to a simple-minded precision dance with everyone kicking up at the same time, twirling in unison and bowing off en masse, but to an intricate ballet in which the individual dancers and ensembles all have distinctive parts which miraculously reinforce each other and compose an orderly whole. The ballet of the good city sidewalk never repeats itself from place to place, and in any one place is always replete with new improvisations.

The stretch of Hudson Street where I live is each day the scene of an intricate sidewalk ballet. I make my own first entrance into it a little after eight when I put out the garbage can, surely a prosaic occupation, but I enjoy my part, my little clang, as the droves of junior high school students walk by the center of the stage dropping candy wrappers. (How do they eat so much candy so early in the morning?)

While I sweep up the wrappers I watch the other rituals of morning: Mr. Halpert unlocking the laundry's handcart from its mooring to a cellar door, Joe Cornacchia's son-in-law stacking out the empty crates from the delicatessen, the barber bringing out his sidewalk folding chair, Mr. Goldstein arranging the coils of wire which proclaim the hardware store is open, the wife of the tenement's superintendent depositing her chunky three-year-old with a toy mandolin on the stoop, the vantage point from which he is learning the English his mother cannot speak. Now the primary children, heading for St. Luke's, dribble through to the south; the children for St. Veronica's cross, heading to the west, and the children for P.S. 41, heading toward the east. Two new entrances are being made from the wings: well-dressed and even elegant women and men with brief cases emerge from doorways and side streets. Most of these are heading for the bus and subways, but some hover on the curbs, stopping taxis which have miraculously appeared at the right moment, for the taxis are part of a wider morning ritual: having dropped passengers from midtown in the downtown financial district, they are now bringing downtowners up to midtown. Simultaneously, numbers of women in housedresses have emerged and as they crisscross with one another they pause for quick conversations that sound with either laughter or joint indignation, never, it seems, anything between. It is time for me to hurry to work too, and I exchange my ritual farewell with Mr. Lofaro, the short, thick-bodied, white-aproned fruit man who stands outside his doorway a little up the street, his arms folded, his feet planted, looking solid as earth itself. We nod; we each glance quickly up and down the street, then look back to each other and smile. We have done this many a morning for more than ten years, and we both know what it means: All is well.

The heart-of-the-day ballet I seldom see, because part of the nature of it is that working people who live there, like me, are mostly gone, filling the roles of strangers on other sidewalks. But from days off, I know enough of it to know that it becomes more and more intricate. Longshoremen who are not working that day gather at the White Horse or the Ideal or the International for beer and conversation. The executives and business lunchers from the industries just to the west throng the Dorgene restaurant and the Lion's Head coffee house; meat-market workers and communications scientists fill the bakery lunchroom. Character dancers come on, a strange old man with strings of old shoes over his shoulders, motor-scooter riders with big beards and girl friends who bounce on the back of the scooters and wear their hair long in front of their faces as well as behind, drunks who follow the advice of the Hat Council and are always turned out in hats, but not hats the Council would approve. Mr. Lacey, the locksmith, shuts up his shop for a while and goes to exchange the time of day with Mr. Slube at the cigar store. Mr. Koochagian, the tailor, waters the luxuriant jungle of plants in his window, gives them a critical look from the outside, accepts a compliment on them from two passers-by, fingers the leaves on the plane tree in front of our house with a thoughtful gardener's appraisal, and crosses the street for a bite at the Ideal where he can keep an eye on customers and wigwag across the message that he is coming. The baby carriages come out, and clusters of everyone from toddlers with dolls to teen-agers with homework gather at the stoops.

When I get home after work, the ballet is reaching its crescendo. This is the time of roller skates and stilts and tricycles, and games in the lee of the stoop with bottletops and plastic cowboys; this is the time of bundles and packages, zigzagging from the drug store to the fruit stand and back over to the butcher's; this is the time when teen-agers, all dressed up, are pausing to ask if their slips show or their collars look right; this is the time when beautiful girls get out of MG's; this is the time when the fire engines go through; this is the time when anybody you know around Hudson Street will go by.

As darkness thickens and Mr. Halpert moors the laundry cart to the cellar door again, the ballet goes on under lights, eddying back and forth but intensifying at the bright spotlight pools of Joe's sidewalk pizza dispensary, the bars, the delicatessen, the restaurant and the drug store. The night workers stop now at the delicatessen, to pick up salami and a container of milk. Things have settled down for the evening but the street and its ballet have not come to a stop.

I know the deep night ballet and its seasons best from waking long after midnight to tend a baby and, sitting in the dark, seeing the shadows and hearing the sounds of the sidewalk. Mostly it is a sound like infinitely pattering snatches of party conversation and, about three in the morning, singing, very good singing. Sometimes there is sharpness and anger or sad, sad weeping, or a flurry of search for a string of beads broken. One night a young man came roaring along, bellowing terrible language at two girls whom he had apparently picked up and who were disappointing him. Doors opened, a wary semicircle formed around him, not too close, until the police came. Out came the heads, too, along Hudson Street, offering opinion, "Drunk . . . Crazy . . . A wild kid from the suburbs."[2]

Deep in the night, I am almost unaware how many people are on the street unless something calls them together, like the bagpipe. Who the piper was and why he favored our street I have no idea. The bagpipe just skirled out in the February night, and as if it were a signal the random, dwindled movements of the sidewalk took on direction. Swiftly, quietly, almost magically a little crowd was there, a crowd that evolved into a circle with a Highland fling inside it. The crowd could be seen on the shadowy sidewalk, the dancers could be seen, but the bagpiper himself was almost invisible because his bravura was all in his music. He was a very little man in a plain brown overcoat. When he finished and vanished, the dancers and watchers applauded, and applause came from the galleries too, half a dozen of the hundred windows on Hudson Street. Then the windows closed, and the little crowd dissolved into the random movements of the night street.

[2] He turned out to be a wild kid from the suburbs. Sometimes, on Hudson Street, we are tempted to believe the suburbs must be a difficult place to bring up children.

The strangers on Hudson Street, the allies whose eyes help us natives keep the peace of the street, are so many that they always seem to be different people from one day to the next. That does not matter. Whether they are so many always-different people as they seem to be, I do not know. Likely they are. When Jimmy Rogan fell through a plate-glass window (he was separating some scuffling friends) and almost lost his arm, a stranger in an old T shirt emerged from the Ideal bar, swiftly applied an expert tourniquet and, according to the hospital's emergency staff, saved Jimmy's life. Nobody remembered seeing the man before and no one has seen him since. The hospital was called in this way: a woman sitting on the steps next to the accident ran over to the bus stop, wordlessly snatched the dime from the hand of a stranger who was waiting with his fifteen-cent fare ready, and raced into the Ideal's phone booth. The stranger raced after her to offer the nickel too. Nobody remembered seeing him before, and no one has seen him since. When you see the same stranger three or four times on Hudson Street, you begin to nod. This is almost getting to be an acquaintance, a public acquaintance, of course.

I have made the daily ballet of Hudson Street sound more frenetic than it is, because writing it telescopes it. In real life, it is not that way. In real life, to be sure, something is always going on, the ballet is never at a halt, but the general effect is peaceful and the general tenor even leisurely. People who know well such animated city streets will know how it is. I am afraid people who do not will always have it a little wrong in their heads—like the old prints of rhinoceroses made from travelers' descriptions of rhinoceroses.

On Hudson Street, the same as in the North End of Boston or in any other animated neighborhoods of great cities, we are not innately more competent at keeping the sidewalks safe than are the people who try to live off the hostile truce of Turf in a blind-eyed city. We are the lucky possessors of a city order that makes it relatively simple to keep the peace because there are plenty of eyes on the street. But there is nothing simple about that order itself, or the bewildering number of components that go into it. Most of those components are specialized in one way or another. They unite in their joint effect upon the sidewalk, which is not specialized in the least. That is its strength.

The Need for Community Among Negroes

JOHN SLAWSON

Especially in periods of crisis and change, most men have usually conceptualized issues in terms of *either/or* rather than *both/and* solutions. Throughout the late nineteenth and early twentieth centuries, for instance, the solution to the economic problem was usually seen in terms of *either* socialism *or* capitalism, state control *or* free enterprise. Fortunately, in actual practice rather than ideologically, the Welfare State has proved to be a tentative and everchanging *both/and* solution, combining as much free enterprise as possible with as much state regulation as has been necessary.

And so it has been with ideological proposals for the solution of the problem of Negro-white relations in America. Ever since Emancipation, as Howard Brotz, a sociologist quoted in this selection, has written, "there has been a tension between the quest for autonomy—moral, cultural, political—of the Negro as a people or a community *and* the quest for the right to be integrated as individuals into a multiracial, universalistic society." In the long run, the tension will probably be overcome, like the economic problem, by *both* community building *and* integration. Nevertheless, in the short run some will emphasize one and some the other. In the recent past, the civil rights movement, and most men of good will who have supported it, has stressed the need for integration—and has incidentally created a new and capable Negro leadership with ever stronger ties to a more and more self-conscious Negro community. John Slawson, in this selection, reviews the history of Negro-white relations in the light of a possible need today for an increased emphasis on community building.

Reprinted from *Commentary,* "Mutual Aid and the Negro," April, 1966, by permission; copyright © 1966, by the American Jewish Committee.

I

THE IDEA OF SELF-HELP OR MUTUAL AID AS A MEANS TO FURTHER progress in securing full equality is not, to put it mildly, popular among Negroes. As the recent White House conference on civil rights made clear, Negroes tend to have three basic objections to the idea. First of all, they see the emphasis on self-help as a diversionary tactic, either consciously or unconsciously motivated by a desire on the part of whites to shift attention from the real issue of discrimination in employment, housing, and schools, to the putative deficiencies or weaknesses of the Negro community and the Negro family. A second objection, flowing directly out of the first, is that the emphasis on self-help is only a covert way of implying that the Negro bears an important share in the responsibility for his own plight. And finally, there is the objection pointedly formulated not long ago in these pages by Bayard Rustin:

> I would advise those who think that self-help is the answer to familiarize themselves with the long history of such efforts in the Negro community, and to consider why so many foundered on the shoals of ghetto life.

Now there is no question that certain white advocates of Negro self-help—I am thinking particularly of John Fischer and Eric Hoffer—have discussed the matter in such a way as to lend substance to these objections. To say, as Mr. Fischer did, for example, that "So long as the Negro blames his plight entirely on circumstances, history and the white man, he's going to stay in that plight," is to invite a justifiably hostile response. For the truth is that prejudice is never a consequence of the actions or characteristics of the victim; it comes from the bigot himself (who, to be sure, will always rationalize his feelings by pegging them to the victim's "objectionable" traits). In any case, however, if the issue is one of distributing *blame,* then the white man does indeed deserve it, and "entirely," to use Mr. Fischer's word. But the issue, of course, is not the distribution of blame: the issue is jobs, housing, and schools. The $100-billion "freedom budget" proposed by A. Philip Randolph and the massive housing and job-training programs advocated by various civil rights organizations are the answer to the problem of family instability among Negroes which the much-abused Moynihan Report has focused so much attention upon, just as they are the answer to the "Dull, Devastating Spiral of Failure" which the McCone Report on the Watts riots discusses at such great length. To quote Rustin again: "If Negroes suffer more than others from the problem of family instability today, it is not because they are Negro but because they are so disproportionately unemployed, underemployed, and ill-paid." So long as we have Negro ghettos, just so long will the main order of business be to break them down, with all that breaking them down implies.

Nevertheless, while crash programs directed at this objective must have priority and are a necessary condition for securing "equality as a fact and not just as a right," they are not in themselves a sufficient one. In implying that they are, Rustin and others permit themselves to lose sight, at least temporarily, of the important truth that there are things that no one can do for a man except the man himself. Mutual aid—which is to say, true self-help—as Rustin rightly points out, is not the same thing as self-improvement. In the last analysis—and particularly in a period when the government is more and more supplanting private philanthropy as the main support of welfare and economic-opportunity programs—mutual aid is more valuable as a means of building a sense of community, of group solidarity and individual pride, than as a technique (which it traditionally was) for dealing with the problems of the poor. One need only look at the civil rights movement, especially since 1954, to see what a powerful force for the creation of group pride the doing-for-oneself can be. And there is some impressive evidence to show that the relevance of such pride to the goal of integration is more direct than it may at first glance appear. Thus, reporting in his *Strangers Next Door* on a study of interracial social contact, Professor Robin Williams of Cornell writes:

> Respondents who manifest a militant group pride are significantly more likely to have interracial social contact than non-militants and, conversely, those who score high in group self-hatred clearly tend to have less contact than those who are relatively lacking in self-hatred. In other words, it is the individual who identifies positively with his racial group who is likely to have interracial contact.

Mutual aid, then, would seem to be inherently desirable from every point of view. Yet many Negroes, even if it is urged upon them *not* as a diversion but rather as a complementary process to programs of outside assistance, still resist the idea. Why? For an answer to this question, one could do worse than follow Rustin's advice and examine "the long history of such efforts in the Negro community"—but not only "to consider why so many foundered on the shoals of ghetto life." One must also seek to understand the effect these founderings have had on the internal condition of the Negro community today.

II

As with so much else, the natural human impulse for social organization and mutual help was from the earliest days of plantation life stifled among Negroes by punitive legislation. In the Caribbean slave codes (which were incorporated into American colonial law and then into state law), for example, the assembling of more than four or five slaves was forbidden except when a white person was present. Moreover, the Black Codes saw to it that a slave who shared his troubles with fellow slaves would only bring new troubles upon himself. Slavery thus largely succeeded in destroying the sense of community and of shared fate among Negroes. A white visitor in Virginia in 1856 observed that the slave master destroyed "the sympathy that unites . . . the victims of the same oppression. . . . He has but to arm the human passions against each other."

In 1776, slavery was legal in all the colonies, but by 1830 it had been abolished in the Northern states. The number of slaves grew from a half million before the Revolution to over two million in 1830. Free Negroes increased from 40,000 in 1776 to 320,000 in 1830, 57 per cent of them—surprisingly—living in the slave states. These free Negroes in the South followed a more hazardous existence than in the North, for they could more easily be returned into slavery; nevertheless, they organized themselves from the earliest days of the Republic. The Brown Fellowship Society, founded in Charleston, South Carolina in November 1790, was the first Negro mutual-aid society. But coming into being in a world of caste, it was as caste-conscious as the white slaveholders themselves: thus, membership was restricted to mulattoes and quadroons, and "black men were not eligible." The following year, however, free black Negroes in Charleston formed a society of their own called the Free Dark Men of Color. Both groups gave help to their members: relief to poor widows, educational assistance to orphans, a cemetery and burial. Both maintained clubhouses for social purposes, and both set high standards for moral conduct and social behavior—in conformity, of course, with the ideals of the white world.

In other Southern cities with substantial groups of free Negroes, similar societies came into existence: New Orleans, Richmond, Washington, Baltimore, and St. Petersburg, Florida. But after the Nat Turner insurrection of 1831, in which sixty whites were killed, a series of laws was enacted which struck the first major blow to the development of communal association among free Negroes. They were denied the right of assembly; they could not hold church services without the presence of a licensed white minister; and they were prohibited from visiting or entertaining slaves and from convening meetings of benevolent societies and other organizations. In Maryland, free Negroes could not have "lyceums, lodges, fire companies, or literary, dramatic, social, moral, or charitable societies." In many slave states, they were enjoined from engaging in certain occupations and from trading in certain commodities.

De Tocqueville shrewdly observed that "the prejudice of race appears to be stronger in the states that have abolished slavery than in those where it still exists; and nowhere is it so intolerant as in those states where servitude has never been known." Nevertheless, in the North, free Negroes began early to organize mutual-aid and self-improvement societies. The very first was the Free African Society, founded in Philadelphia in 1787 by Richard Allen, a self-taught Methodist preacher who "worked out" to buy his own liberty. The society undertook to build a fund for mutual aid, to help its members look after their sick, to care for their poor widows and educate their orphans, and to bury their dead. It adopted resolutions to strengthen marriage bonds and familial responsibility, and it provided for the suspension of members guilty of drunkenness or disorderly conduct.

Although mutual-aid and church groups also came into being among free Negroes in other Northern cities (Boston in 1796, and New York in 1808), it was in Philadelphia that an organized free Negro community had its most impressive unfolding. Philadelphia, in the early decades of the nineteenth-century, benefited from the presence of a group of Negroes with exceptional gifts of leadership, some of whose families had enjoyed several generations of freedom—a wealthy industrialist, a bishop, an editor and publisher, an orator. They were a unique elite among free Negroes, and together they stimulated and set in motion a variety of Negro associations and activities ranging from temperance societies and relief work to anti-slavery conventions. Their activities, though on a more modest scale, bring to mind the communal and philanthropic efforts of the acculturated German Jews in America at the end of the nineteenth and early twentieth centuries on behalf of the East-European Jewish immigrants then streaming into the United States.

According to W. E. B. Du Bois's pioneering sociological study *The Philadelphia Negro* (published in 1889), about 7,000 Philadelphia Negroes were members of a hundred mutual-aid societies in 1838; ten years later these societies claimed about 8,000 members. (The figures seem inflated; the 1850 census reported 10,700 free Negroes in Philadelphia, but even so, free Negroes in Philadelphia had an impressive record of communal associations.)

Philadelphia, too, was where the Negro Convention Movement started in 1830. Organized first to protest Ohio's renewed rigid enforcement of an old fugitive-slave law (as a consequence, about a thousand Negroes migrated from Ohio to Canada), the movement developed on a national scale and in many free states, combining abolitionism with self-improvement and moral uplift. The appeal of the first Negro convention reminded Negro freemen "that knowledge is power, and to that end, we call on you to sustain and support, by all honorable, energetic, and necessary means, those presses which are devoted to our instruction and elevation, to foster and encourage the mechanical arts and sciences among our brethren, to encourage simplicity, neatness, temperance, and economy in our habits." Two years later, the national convention reported that temperance societies had been organized in several states and that plans for manual-labor schools in New York and in Philadelphia were under way.

But as repressive legislation stifled Negro organization in the South, the rising tide of Irish and German immigration, and the violent encounter between the Negroes and the new immigrants, rudely shattered the brilliant promise of an organized free Negro community in early nineteenth-century Philadelphia. Anti-Negro riots began in 1829 and did not subside until after the Civil War. (In New York the Civil War itself was the occasion for the violently anti-Negro draft riots.) In 1836, Philadelphia Negroes even lost the right to vote—a right which they had possessed since 1790. It was "a time of retrogression for the mass of the race," wrote Du Bois. The Negro leadership was trapped between the prejudice and violence of the whites and the unmanageable, ever-growing mass of fugitive Southern Negroes streaming into the city.

That migration of illiterate and occupationally untrained Negroes before the Civil War, inundating the established communities of Northern Negroes, was a foretaste of the dislocation that was to come after the Civil War. On the eve of the Civil War there were almost 500,000 free Negroes in the United States, and four million Negro slaves. Only a small proportion of slaves had been trained as craftsmen (carpenters, coopers, tailors, shoemakers, bootmakers, cabinetmakers, plasterers); others had labored in salt works, mines, on railroad construction and docks; but most had no experience beyond the cotton fields or domestic service. The vast majority were totally without education (according to the 1870 census, 80 per cent of non-whites in America were illiterate). The experience of free Negroes with associations for mutual aid and self-improvement had been fragile in the South, hardier and somewhat more durable in the North, but in North and South alike that experience had largely been confined to Negroes who possessed some education, skills, and means.

The havoc of the Civil War, the emancipation of the slaves, and the consequent disorganization of Southern society, had the effect of submerging these comparatively advantaged free Negroes in the vast sea of newly freed slaves, limiting their opportunities for economic and educational advancement, and reducing their capacity for independent leadership. As for the ex-slaves themselves, without financial or material resources, without skills or literacy, they were thrust into conditions of unparalleled misery.

To be sure, the Bureau of Refugees, Freedmen, and Abandoned Land—established in 1865 and probably the first federal agency to assume responsibility for the welfare and protection of large numbers of the population—provided some help. But its main work ceased in 1869, and its only lasting legacy of achievement was the founding of several outstanding Negro educational institutions: Howard University, Hampton Institute, Atlanta University, Fisk University. By contrast, the Freedmen's Bank, set up by the federal government for Negroes, but operated by a private group, left only a legacy of mistrust and despair among Negroes whose scanty savings were dissipated—and never repaid—in mismanagement, speculation, and deceit.

In 1872, the Freedmen's Bureau ceased all operations. Five years later, the last federal troops withdrew from Louisiana and South Carolina. Reconstruction governments which had stood between the Negroes and whites were dissolved or overthrown. Without the military power and the civilian presence of the federal government, Negroes in the South remained without resources, without friends or allies. Thus, instead of a national effort being launched to make self-reliant citizens of the ex-slaves, all Negroes in the South were consigned to a marginal existence.

After Reconstruction, destitute thousands began an exodus out of the South looking for a land of freedom in the North and West. In 1879 alone, some 40,000 migrated. The resources of the few private relief agencies were inadequate to cope with this flood, but though Congress investigated and debated the question of aid to the migrant freedman, it never enacted any legislation. As for the millions of Negroes who remained in the South, a new era of disenfranchisement and segregation awaited them: Jim-Crow legislation solidified Southern prejudice in a rigid and unyielding caste system; law and custom contrived for them an existence of poverty and humiliation.

In 1898, Du Bois published one of his first sociological studies under the auspices of Atlanta University, *Some Efforts of Negroes for Their Own Social Betterment.* Using materials collected by his students, Du Bois extolled the scope and variety of organized activity among Negroes:

> . . . there are among them 23,000 churches, with unusually wide activities, and spending annually at least $10,000,000. There are

> thousands of secret societies with their insurance and social features, large numbers of beneficial societies with their economic and benevolent cooperation. . . . Finally there are the slowly evolving organs by which the group seeks to stop and minimize the antisocial deeds and accidents of its members. This is a picture of all human striving—unusually simple, with local and social peculiarities, but strikingly human and worth further study and attention.[1]

Du Bois appears to have exaggerated the extent and stability of Negro association. He used his sources uncritically, because he was exploiting scientific study for defensive purposes, painting the reality larger than life. Though the Negro churches expanded with enormous rapidity and commanded the deep loyalty of Negro masses, they were often too poor in organizational and intellectual resources to develop stable self-help activities, and too much directed to the next world to build self-reliance in this one. As for the mushrooming fraternal orders, mutual-benefit and insurance societies, most were small, circumscribed, and short-lived. Undoubtedly, the regalia and ceremonials provided their members with an opportunity to escape the humiliations and hardships of the real world and to enjoy companionship and congeniality. But "loosely organized and poorly managed, with few or no regulations placed upon the officials, no controls, no actuarial studies," many organizations failed, unable to meet their obligations.[2] These failures, in the wake of the more spectacular failure of the Freedmen's Bank, discouraged the growth of associations for mutual aid among Negroes. They appeared to be—as they indeed were—incompetent, unreliable, and abusive of their financial trust, and they have left a heritage of suspicion among Negroes toward organizations for mutual aid.

III

Not the least important of the failures of these societies and churches is the fact that none of them produced a Negro leader of national or even regional stature. This, combined with the abdication of the federal government, meant that the first generation out of slavery—untrained for the newer industrial occupations and economically crushed in the competition for livelihood between the emergent poor whites in the South and the European immigrants in the North—not only had to combat prejudice and discrimination on their own, but also had to try, unaided,

[1] Quoted from John Hope Franklin, *From Slavery to Freedom: A History of American Negroes.*

[2] Robert H. Kinzer and Edward Sagarin, *The Negro in American Business: The Conflict Between Separatism and Integration.*

to surmount their educational, social, and cultural disabilities, the product of generations of slavery.

A small number of this first generation out of slavery succeeded in true Horatio Alger fashion. Such a one was Booker T. Washington, the first authentic Negro leader of national stature to emerge in the post-Reconstruction era, and about whom Du Bois said in 1903: "Easily the most striking thing in the history of the American Negro since 1876 is the ascendancy of Mr. Booker T. Washington."[3]

The peak of Washington's national renown and acceptance by whites as a Negro leader came in his celebrated address in 1895 at the opening of the Cotton States Exposition in Atlanta. That five-minute speech, in which Washington expressed his philosophy of race relations at that juncture in American history, served also to solidify rising militant Negro opposition to him. He began with a simple literary device:

> A ship lost at sea for many days suddenly sighted a friendly vessel. From the mast of the unfortunate vessel was seen a signal, "Water, water; we die of thirst!" The answer from the friendly vessel at once came back, "Cast down your bucket where you are." A second time the signal, "Water, water; send us water!" ran up from the distressed vessel, and was answered, "Cast down your bucket where you are." And a third and fourth signal for water was answered, "Cast down your bucket where you are." The captain of the distressed vessel, at last heeding the injunction, cast down his bucket, and it came up full of fresh, sparkling water from the mouth of the Amazon River.[4]

"Cast down your bucket where you are" constituted an admonition to Negroes to abandon ideas of emigration and to cultivate friendly relations with white Southerners: Negroes, Washington urged, should turn to basic occupations "in agriculture, mechanics, in commerce, in domestic service, and in the professions," for "it is at the bottom of life we must begin, and not at the top." But "Cast down your bucket where you are" also constituted an admonition to white Southerners to use Negro manpower in agriculture and industry instead of "those of foreign birth and strange tongue and habits." The Negro, said Washington, felt a devotion to the white South "that no foreigner can approach," and he emphasized the historically close relations between the races and their common purposes. Yet lest he be misunderstood—this was Atlanta in 1895, when segregation had already become solidified in Jim-Crow legis-

[3] "On Mr. Booker T. Washington and others," *The Souls of Black Folk,* in John Hope Franklin, ed., *Three Negro Classics.*

[4] Booker T. Washington, *Up From Slavery: An Autobiography.*

lation—he added: "In all things that are purely social we can be as separate as the fingers, yet one as the hand in all things essential to mutual progress." And on another occasion, decrying the agitation for social equality as "the extremist folly," he declared: "It is important and right that all privileges of the law be ours, but it is vastly more important that we be prepared for the exercises of these privileges. The opportunity to earn a dollar in a factory just now is worth infinitely more than the opportunity to spend a dollar in an opera-house."

Booker T. Washington, the spokesman for Southern rural Negroes barely a generation out of slavery, knew the disabilities of the people from whom he had emerged. He evolved a social and educational policy for the Negro masses which was intended to turn them into productive agricultural and industrial plebs. That policy began with what the principal at Hampton Institute had called "the gospel of the toothbrush," and included the use of bed sheets, the repair of torn and broken articles, the practice of cleanliness, thrift, and sobriety. (One is reminded of Abraham Cahan, editor of the Socialist *Jewish Daily Forward,* who made the use of the handkerchief a central article in his program for the Russian Jewish immigrants.) Washington believed it was to the advantage of the Negro masses to concentrate primarily on self-improvement and vocational training. He had hopes, or visions, that Negroes, once having shed the educational and psychological disabilities of slavehood, and disciplined and hardened by the practice of Protestant virtues, would eventually be accepted as civic, if not social, equals.

The often-repeated charge that Washington represented "the old attitude of adjustment and submission" to the racist South originated among Northern college-educated Negro intellectuals—the radicals of the Niagara Movement, whose social, educational, and professional aspirations extended far beyond Washington's modest goals for the rural masses. Their view was given wide currency in Gunnar Myrdal's *An American Dilemma,* which termed Washington's philosophy "accommodation" and Du Bois's "protest." More recently, Howard Brotz, taking a fresh look at this controversy in *The Black Jews of Harlem,* described it as "a tension between the quest for autonomy—moral, cultural, political—of the American Negro as a people or a community [Washington], *and* the quest for the right to be integrated as individuals into a multiracial, universalistic society [Du Bois]."

This tension was a by-product of the stratification in socioeconomic status among Negroes that was developing between 1890 and 1914. Negroes whose families had been free for several generations, or who had lived in the North for several generations, formed the core of a slowly expanding elite of college-educated professionals and businessmen, now numerous enough to constitute a full-fledged segment of Negro society—a social and economic group, rather than a mere handful of individuals. Out of this group came the Radicals. For themselves and aspirants to their class, the Radicals demanded a different educational policy from that which Washington advocated for the masses. Washington put his greatest emphasis on elementary and industrial education; they insisted on higher education. Du Bois himself, born in Great Barrington, Massachusetts, and educated at Harvard (one undergraduate year at Fisk was his first exposure to Southern Negro life), advocated an elitist philosophy—education for the "Talented Tenth," to develop "the Best of this race that they may guide the Mass away from the contamination and death of the Worst."

Washington had wanted to build an economically self-reliant community that could survive in autonomous self-sufficiency. (His main error, perhaps, was that his ideas were better suited to a pre-industrial than an industrial economy, and to the pre-Jim Crow society in which they originally took shape.) The Radicals wanted total assimilation and total integration, including social acceptance in white society. (The rebuffs with which they met led them to occasional flirtations with pan-African nationalism, but at heart they adhered to their assimilatory purposes.) Out of this latter program two organizations, both interracial, came into being in the first decade of the twentieth century: the NAACP and the National Urban League, the former politically radical, the latter more staid. The NAACP made its goal the achievement of equality before the law; the Urban League began as a social-welfare agency to help the Negro migrant adjust to the conditions of the Northern urban industrial and commercial centers. The Negroes in both organizations were nearly all Northern, college-educated, and more closely identified with white professionals and communal leaders than with other Negroes. Indeed, they had more acceptance from that white world than from the Negro masses, who did not—and to a surprising extent still do not—know them. Washington's leadership, in contrast, had rested on two bases—support from the mass of Southern rural Negroes and recognition by white political leaders. (With his death, Southern rural Negroes remained leaderless until the emergence in 1955 of Martin Luther King as a national figure.)

During World War I, Negro migration from the South to Northern industrial cities accelerated. Poor, ill-educated, untrained for industrial occupations, friendless and disoriented, the new migrants had no interest in, or benefit from, the NAACP's program, and the National Urban League was not yet in a position to help them. These urban Negro masses found their leader in Marcus Garvey, the Black Moses. A Jamaican who came to the United States in 1916 as head of the Universal Negro Improvement Association, he preached with spectacular success a doctrine of black nationalism and racial pride in African origins. At the movement's peak in 1920–21, Garvey was reputed to have had at least a half million members (some think even a million), and he raised more money than any Negro organization had ever dreamed of. The key to Garvey's appeal was that he exalted everything that was black. Black stood for strength and beauty; Christ, he said, was black and Moses was black. Garvey preached that Negroes must renounce all hope of assistance from whites. The Negroes' only hope was to leave this country of oppression and return to Africa. The Negro intellectuals hated Garvey, dismayed by the anti-white sentiments he articulated, for their expectations were based on cooperation with whites. But Garvey's followers came from the lower classes. He "put steel in the spine of many Negroes," developed race pride and compensation for feelings of inferiority.

Still, Garvey's Universal Negro Improvement Association expired in shame. Garvey was convicted of using the mails to defraud through raising money for his Black Star steamship line, though it is more likely that he himself was victim rather than victimizer. Sentenced to Atlanta Penitentiary, he was later deported as an undesirable alien to the West Indies, where he died. He left a dual legacy, an experience that reinforced lower-class Negro distrust of organizations that dissipated their funds, but also an exhilarating discovery of race pride through black nationalism. Today's Black Muslims are the natural heirs of the Garvey movement. (Elijah Muhammad, indeed, once paid tribute to Garvey as a "very fine Muslim.")

Booker T. Washington, W. E. B. Du Bois, and Marcus Garvey were the outstanding exponents of the three major goals in Negro life: communal self-improvement, the struggle for legal equality, and race pride. Nowadays no Negro organization is dedicated exclusively to one or another of these purposes; all three strands are intertwined. The struggle for civil rights has out of its own inner dynamics bred a wider sense of community among Negroes, and helped to develop a more inclusive social policy. Negroes are now a community in the making, but a community which has not yet overcome its heritage of imposed divisiveness, and its history of frail and discouraging associational experiences. This community needs a stable political, social, and educational policy that will serve the needs of all, not just of a Talented Tenth. Can the existing organizations develop such a policy out of their own heritage of group associations?

IV

The "egocentric predicament," Ralph Barton Perry's phrase for men's inability to see the world except through their own eyes, explains some of the difficulties in communication among America's ethnic, racial, and religious groups. Each group regards the other from the perspective of its own experience and its own culture, and for this reason Jews have understandably been the group with the highest, and perhaps most unrealistic, expectations of Negroes in terms of self-help and communal organization. From Talmudic times on, Jews evolved a communal structure designed to maintain themselves as a distinct group and to transmit their religious culture from generation to generation; and this tradition was carried over to America. Thus the medieval *hekdesh* to care for the sick was translated in America into a great network of Jewish hospitals; the UJA fulfills the *mitzvot* of caring for the needy and redeeming the captives; the ORT continues to enable the poor to become vocationally self-reliant (in Maimonides's view, the highest degree of charity). So pervasive has the habit of philanthropy among Jews become that even country clubs require prospective members to make substantial contributions to UJA as a concrete expression of their identity with the congregation of Israel.

All communal organization is based on a "we feeling," an expanded family solidarity, and attachment to a shared culture. The crucial factor in successful organization of *formal* institutions is past experience in self-government, whereas simple and informal communal institutions may require little more than the "we feeling," the desire to maintain group cohesion. The Italian immigrants to America, for example, had little sense of a shared national Italian culture or of belonging to a national Italian polity, but the extended family sufficed to protect them against the stresses of the outer society. Loyalty to the family has remained the cornerstone of Italian group solidarity in the absence of formal communal institutions. Their economic attainments and their dominance in certain occupations—construction and sanitation are two such—have largely been the consequence of group cohesion and familial connections.

Among the Irish, group cohesion was nurtured by their history of English-Anglican oppression, by an assured and aggressive Church with its parochial school system, by a prodigious sense of self-esteem, and a host of informal communal institutions. Among Greeks, fraternal societies served to preserve and develop a sense of communal belonging: those societies gave financial help to relatives and friends who remained behind in Greece, and they served to organize the American Greek community in support of the home country's political causes. The Chinese, too, maintained an extensive and interlocking network of benevolent, mutual-aid, and communal institutions, ranging from temples and churches to language schools and hospitals. Excluded from many occupations by state laws and labor unions, the Chinese went into businesses that might give them economic independence and they attained signal success in two fields closely related to domestic service, above which they desired to rise: laundries and restaurants.

The communal structures of these different ethnic and racial groups developed out of cultures which set a high value on the group's preservation and whose traditions of "self-government" the immigrants could adapt to their respective situations in America. Negroes have been largely deprived of any such experience of self-government by the particular forms of oppression to which they have been subjected. What they have is a history of fragile communal organization battered by repressive legislation and group divisiveness; and they have further been weakened as a community by the failure of middle-class Negroes "to play the role of a responsible elite," as the late E. Franklin Frazier put it in his classic work *Black Bourgeoisie*. The Negro middle class, although relatively small (an estimated 26 per cent of the Negro population as compared with 64 per cent of the whites), nevertheless includes an expanding number of persons.[5] Yet only a handful of those at its topmost echelon (the one hundred wealthiest, listed in the May 1962 issue of *Ebony*) are on the boards of the National Urban League or the NAACP; nor, it would seem, have those below this economic level been notable for their philanthropic concern with fellow Negroes.

This traditional weakness in communal structure is perhaps an even more serious handicap today—when the economic gap is widening not only between Negroes and whites, but also between the Negro middle class and the Negro masses—than it ever was. But tradition is not a static phenomenon; and while it cannot be imposed from without, new cultural patterns can be forged from within when the will to establish them exists, as now seems to be the case to a greater extent than previously among the Negro middle class. Thus, all the major Negro organizations are nowadays engaged in some self-help projects (while carefully avoiding that designation). As one might expect from its history, the

[5] Between 1950 and 1960, for example, there was a threefold increase in the number of Negro engineers; the number of architects increased 72 per cent, natural scientists, 77 per cent, lawyers, 43 per cent, dentists, 31 per cent, and physicians, 14 per cent. Overall, some 300,000 Negroes have been added to this class since 1940.

Urban League is foremost among them—concerning itself with family problems, home and neighborhood improvement, vocational guidance and back-to-school programs for the young—but the NAACP recently also began to move into this field, organizing "Citizenship Clinics" in the North. Then, too, there is the recent growth of savings-and-loan associations owned and operated by Negroes (Elmer M. Lancaster of the Department of Commerce calls this one of the most significant factors in the American economy). And finally, on the national scale, there are agencies like the National Council of Negro Women and the National Business League.

Apart from the major organizations, we also find hundreds of small, local efforts of a more or less informal character. There are "The Leaguers" in Newark, New Jersey, an organization for Negro teen-agers founded sixteen years ago by Mrs. Mary Burch, an educator and social worker, to stimulate and encourage Negro teen-agers to continue their education through college and also to teach youngsters self-reliance through community service. The United Credit Union, established in Watts about a year before the riots, is now the center of self-help activity in the area, many residents having lost their jobs in the wake of the riots, and small-loan companies having tightened up credit to Watts residents. Finally, there are such projects as "Operation Upgrade" (in Bedford-Stuyvesant), and the Morningside Parents Association and the New Era Neighborhood Association (both in Harlem).

What is most interesting and paradoxical about mutual aid among Negroes today, however, is that some of the most effective programs are being carried out by the least likely leaderships—the Black Muslims at one extreme, and at the other, those militant civil rights groups which react with the deepest outrage to the idea of Negro "self-improvement."

Until very recently, the Black Muslims were the only important Negro organization dedicated to self-improvement on a large scale. The Muslim movement has striven for a total transformation of Negro values and traditions. The movement is anti-white, but its moral values are rigidly puritanical and "bourgeois." While the Muslims have succeeded in fashioning a community with high self-regard, they have only been able to do so at the expense of promoting race hatred. Moreover, the Muslim movement is self-defeating, for, as Rustin puts it: ". . . every prostitute the Muslims convert to a model of Calvinist virtue is replaced by the ghetto with two more. Dedicated as they are to maintenance of the ghetto, the Muslims are powerless to effect substantial moral reform."

The paradox underlying self-help among Negroes is most apparent in the militant civil rights groups where but to mention "self-help" is to invite attack. Yet mutual aid is precisely what the militancy of these groups has more and more led them to emphasize in their struggle to win equality. Thus, in Selma, Ala., McComb, Miss., and elsewhere in the heart of Klan territory, Martin Luther King's Southern Christian Leadership Conference and other civil rights organizations have been setting up Negro cooperatives to compensate for economic reprisals against Negroes who have registered to vote—the Poor People's Corporation, cooperative groceries, sewing cooperatives, and other types of business. Thus also, the volunteers in the 1964 Mississippi Summer Program (whose political objective was the Freedom Democratic Party) found themselves involved—almost inevitably—in literacy and tutorial projects in community centers and vocational training. The militant selective boycott program of Philadelphia Negroes to win jobs from big industrial firms made possible the uniquely successful vocational training program (the Opportunities Industrialization Center) conducted by Negro minister Leon Howard Sullivan. Here the *élan* of civil rights activity has carried over into job training: "It's attitude we stress," Sullivan says. "We teach probably 25 per cent skill and 75 per cent attitude. The Negro has got to get his head up and believe in himself."

OIC is now giving special prejob training to some 1,000 Negroes at a time, helping them to brush up on their reading, writing, and arithmetic, and to improve their speech and even their personal grooming. "Many trainees," Sullivan points out, "walk 15 to 20 blocks morning and night to seize the opportunity offered by OIC." Not surprisingly, this enterprise has won the backing of the Philadelphia Chamber of Commerce and the so-called "white power structure." The Office of Manpower, Automation and Training of the U.S. Department of Labor stepped in with a $458,000 grant and the federal anti-poverty program has contributed $1,756,000. But perhaps the most hopeful thing about this project is the fact that Negroes themselves have twice managed to raise $100,000 in city-wide drives to support it.

V

In 1915, the Association for the Study of Negro Life and History was formed as a vehicle through which educated Negroes might rediscover their obscure or forgotten historic traditions. The emphasis was on Negro "contributions": it was a defensive and apologetic emphasis, for educated Negroes (like many Jews) used to be ashamed of their past and wished only to obliterate the memory of submission and accommodation. But as each new generation everywhere revises its view of the past, so, too, are today's younger Negro writers and historians doing: they are coming to see their past—including slavery—not as a sheer humiliation but as a reservoir of dignity and courage in the face of appalling oppression. Ralph Ellison expresses it this way in *Shadow and Act:* "Our Negro situation is changing rapidly, but so much we've gleaned through the harsh discipline of Negro American life is simply too precious to be lost. I speak of the faith, the patience, the humor, the sense of timing, rugged sense of life and the manner of expressing it, which all go to define the American Negro."

A true Negro community is now beginning to emerge out of the civil rights movement. Northern, college-educated young Negroes, in their unique version of populism, in their American-style "going to the people," are expressing solidarity with illiterate Southern Negro sharecroppers, not by rhetoric, but demonstrably by their presence in Alabama and Mississippi. Others are dedicating themselves to serving the Negro poor and outcast in the Northern slums. They are creating new traditions out of which authentic communal associations are developing—traditions as indigenous to the Negro and as relevant to the special complexities of *his* particular condition as immigrant-aid societies and hospitals were to the Jews.

It seems obvious that this is both a necessary and a helpful trend and that everything should be done to further it. No service is performed by those Negro leaders who attack the idea of mutual aid—however understandable the motives behind the attack. When Negro leaders call self-help an Uncle Tom concept, claiming that it implies that Negroes are themselves responsible for their plight and asserting that the responsibility belongs wholly to white society, they may be adopting the right tactic for replying to white people; but what of the impact on the Negroes who overhear? Is it not likely that part of the effect is to dampen Negro initiative, and to help delay the time when the Negro upper and middle class will at last become the "responsible elite" Frazier wanted it to become—earning leadership through a sacrificial involvement in the plight of the Negro mass, deserving it by generous financial contributions to meet communal needs? Would it, then, not be better if, while the primary objective of securing crash programs is being pursued, the newly reawakened impulse toward mutual aid among Negroes were at the same time encouraged and reinforced, instead of derided and decried?

The Church in a New Bohemia

DOUGLAS DAVIS

There has grown up in New York City over the past few years a new bohemian community called the East Village, situated several blocks east along Eighth Street from the older, and now extremely expensive, Greenwich Village. This new bohemia is centered along St. Mark's Place, whose three blocks are lined with old bars, new bars, underground movie houses, dance palaces, and several Russian, German, and Polish churches. Walking along the streets, one sees long-haired boys and girls, dressed alike in leather jackets, Levi's, and Western boots, many inter-racial couples, and a sprinkling of the traditional residents of this low-rent neighborhood, mostly older men and women wearing more conventional clothes and babbling in a variety of foreign tongues. "Perhaps the most distinguishing characteristic of the New Bohemia," writes the art critic John Gruen, "is its acceptance of integration as an unquestioned part of the scene. Young Negroes and Puerto Ricans are part of the crowd at the New Bohemian bars. In fact, they move with apparent ease and security within every field of creative and social activity. It can truly be said that for the New Bohemians every day is Independence Day."

At the heart of this new bohemia stands St. Mark's in-the-Bouwerie, the oldest place of worship on Manhattan Island. This selection shows how the rector of St. Mark's and his parishioners are trying to maintain a continuity of tradition between the Episcopalian establishment and the irreverent young artists, film-makers, and writers who have come to this neighborhood from all over America. Indeed, this ancient church may be participating in some kind of atomic-age Genesis, scandalous to some, creative and utterly appropriate to others. Just as Jane Jacobs (page 74) was able to see, with an artist's eye, a spontaneous order behind the apparent chaos in the street life of lower-class neighborhoods in Boston and

From Douglas Davis, "Is God Dead at St. Mark's in-the-Bouwerie?" in *New York, the World Journal Tribune Magazine,* February 6, 1966, pp. 14, 16, 18, 42. Copyright © 1966 by Douglas Davis. By permission.

New York, so this selection raises the possibility that the chaotic parish life at St. Mark's today may well be anticipating new forms of community in America.

THERE ARE PEOPLE ALL OVER THE ISLAND WHO WILL TELL YOU ALL you want to hear about that maverick church, St. Mark's in-the-Bouwerie, old Christian patriarchs in the substantial Episcopal churches uptown, gentlemen within the Episcopal hierarchy itself, ex-parishioners nursing their private wounds in their brokerage offices. But the ones who really blast off are the neighborhood folks, right around Second Ave. and 10th St., where the old church stands. Go down there sometime and listen to them, old characters of every possible persuasion, drinking in the bars, running the restaurants, staffing the neighborhood law offices. St. Mark's really bothers them, bothers Catholic and Jew as well as Protestant. It hurts these people to see that sweet, old Establishment church, the church that Peter Stuyvesant broke land for before 1660 and Alexander Hamilton defended a century later, the oldest place of worship on the whole island, laid upon by *kids.* Kids staging their Off-Off Broadway plays and showing their underground films and filling up the old churchyard for jazz concerts and political rallies. They'll tell you about it, and they will ask you what happened to the nice, cream-white snobs that used to be Episcopalians. And the ones that have read the big magazines will slam their fists on the bar and bellow those three little words: "Listen to me when I'm telling you. *God is dead* at St. Mark's."

Everything you hear about St. Mark's in the East Village is emotional. The old people rant one way and the kids, the painters and the poets and the film-makers, they rant another. They feel, they *know* that St. Mark's is on their side. Tom Sankey, one of the young OOB playwrights produced at Theatre Genesis, St. Mark's drama wing, says it: "When I used to walk past that old relic on 10th St. I thought of death. Now I think of music and sex and life. You know what our newspaper, *The East Village Other,* called it—'the spirit of the Lower East Side.' " Sankey leaves out the *Other's* concluding message: *"St. Mark's awaits the painters, the writers, the photographers, pornographers, poets, and musicians who care to use its facilities towards their own ends."*

The medieval Christians used to read their sacred writings on three levels—literal, allegorical, tropological. That's the way you have to read St. Mark's, this panting, heaving animal of a church that not long ago lay enfeebled and impotent. On each of the three levels there is a set of people eying the beast in a completely different way. On the outer level are the old guard, the people who read it literally, who want it to be a CHURCH—or at least a landmark. They don't necessarily want to attend it, not even the Episcopalian Fathers. They want to come in from the suburbs and look and sniff and be unafraid. Now they can't do that. Now they stew and fume and choke, because they think the new St. Mark's has something to do with Radical Theology, with the Death of God (their God). On the middle level are the kids, the arty East Village kids, loving St. Mark's as if it were a cool chick come in from Bronxville to warm the bed for a few days, unable to believe that anything so cool and so Establishment could *submit*. . . . Then on the bottom level, close to the real meat, are the True Believers, the people who pay the bills at St. Mark's and mumble the rites and come every Sunday and work like the very devil.

They're pulsating on all three levels. They're all excited about St. Mark's, the enemies and the users and the friends. They know—some dimly, some clearly—that St. Mark's is bringing the news, partly because of where it is and partly because of who is running it, bringing the news about all kinds of things, particularly the Death of God. What none of them sees, what none of them realizes is what Wally Barker knows. He bridges the gap, this 50-year-old painter and vestryman. He has a foot in allegory and a foot in tropology and he interprets the news rightly. "St. Mark's," he says, "is what's happening, don't you see? It's part of the revolution in form everywhere."

The rector of St. Mark's is Michael Allen, a 38-year-old bulldog of a man, with the hardy body, piercing eyes, secular background (a one-time editor at *Look* magazine), and impeccable civil-rights jail record that in sum comprise the union card of the young, liberal cleric. But there is more to him than the card. There are certain paradoxes about him, paradoxes his church shares. Here's this clean-cut young fellow, a High Church man, a self-confessed Calvinist by theology, preaching about sin, holding communion every Sunday, singing sweet the Christian songs, rescuing the old church from death, building up the congregation, holding Bible Study meetings, getting $30,000 from the government to run a community mission over on Avenue D, bringing in the young people to church. In brief, doing a good job. Yet all those plays and films and dirty kids with sandals and paintings. And the nice things he says about the Bishop of Woolwich and Tom Alitzer and Dietrich Bonhoeffer. . . .

The critics listen to the good statistics just so long and then retreat to history. "I'm sick when I pass by St. Mark's." It's an East Village merchant talking. "It's a beautiful old church. What's more, it's a landmark. Do you know the Stuyvesant family is buried there? Now look at it, look at it. They're letting it fall apart so they can put on some dirty plays. Look at the lovely old churchyard. They won't even seed it; the kids play ball on it in the summertime. They had an art show there once and deliberately hung a mobile of busted auto parts right over Peter Stuyvesant's grave. I get sick to look at it."

The Rector sighs when he hears these things. People send him grass seed in the mail, he says, begging him to replant the yard. They should send him money. It would take a quarter of a million dollars to do the job the tourists want done at St. Mark's, to make it a nice landmark. Until he gets his $250,000, and he's trying, the rector's annual budget leans heavily toward the kids and toward community services, by about half, in fact. Until then, the plays and films and sculpture and political rallies and discotheques go on. "We are a microcosm of our world," says the Rector, "and the East Village is our world. I adopt the old Irish Protestant view of the parish. I believe we are here to serve anyone in the parish, not just Episcopalians. The doors of St. Mark's are open to what's happening down here, and the arts are what's happening."

Is God dead? Well, the Rector doesn't say yet. . . .

When you enter the old church you pass through those same three levels. There is on the outside all that stuff the Episcopal Fathers admire, though they don't know that part of it was imported a relatively short time ago. The famous lions of St. Mark's, flanking the center door, were brought in from Italy in the 1920s by the infamous Rector William Norman Guthrie, a collector of profound capacities. There is a huge baptismal font and two Indians on the porch as well, all looking a thousand years old, all shipped here in the '20s.

There are authentic, historically significant graves out in the yard, though—old ones filled with *nice* people: governors and millionaires and a Vice-President of the U.S.A. (Daniel Tompkins, Monroe's man). The Stuyvesants sleep not under a tree, as the old merchant fears, but underneath the church itself. The tourists are reassured by that fact when they can go in through the lions to the nave of St. Mark's, they can *feel* the family down there. They are reassured, too, by the worn old pews and the worn carpets leading down to the altar (they built the naves downhill in the old days). And then above, the balcony, where the slaves used to sit.

When you go in of a Sunday, though, the bustle distracts you. When you invade a service, you're leaving all that literal stuff behind, jumping the middle level, and nosing in with the True Believers. They don't, of course, remind you of the Stuyvesants. Even from the doorway, when all you can see is their backs, you can sense that the Stuyvesants must be itching and rolling about down there, not entirely comfortable. When you look at the new congregation of St. Mark's you see youth, youth black, youth white, dressing like youth, smelling like youth, all around, the heads of the girls bare, tennis shoes, sandals, beards here and there. Plenty of adults, but not the overfed kind. The adults at St. Mark's are lean and spare, the kind of people who have shopped around for a faith, starting, perhaps, with the public lectures at Union Theological Seminary.

Ethel Berger has been a stalwart of St. Mark's since the days shortly after World War II. She remembers how it was. She remembers the day in 1946 when four little old ladies, all white, all Anglo-Saxon, all commuters from out in the suburbs, showed up on Sunday morning. "I was only an occasional communicant myself in the early days. The congregation was an older one, many of whom had moved away from the neighborhood. They came back mainly out of historical obligation, you might say. But the church was dead. Its great old families had gone. There were signs of life later, under Father McEvoy, who actually went out to meet the Negro community. Then, under Michael Allen, life changed. He is very vital and non-restrictive. It's a young group now, many of them artists, and we all work hard. This isn't a social church, it's a working church. There is so much life in the church now between Sunday and Sunday. The arts program has done it, really. I know there's been some criticism of the words these young playwrights use. But I personally have found it very exciting and creative to understand how they feel about things. I don't say, of course, that I approve of everything Theatre Genesis does."

Theatre Genesis is on the middle level, where the kids and the community are, the users of the church. It's this level that divides the congregation from the outsiders. The arts program at St. Mark's—which is at heart Theatre Genesis—is divisive, even now, when the plays have been written about uptown and put on television and called Off-Off Broadway.

The arts program started three years ago. The young rector had wanted to open up the church for the creative people of the East Village for years, but there was no money, hostility in the congregation, no help. Then a young curate named Tom Pike came in who could do the job, and the money was found. When he left, early last year, a layman named Ralph Cook took his place and became Lay Minister for the Arts.

The theater is behind the church and the graveyard, too—round the side to the rear, where stands the brick-and-plaster Parish Hall. You ascend its stairs on a weekday afternoon to the second floor, passing fingerprints and drawings and doodles, and you find, up there, a worn old room with four tiers of seats surrounding a small playing area. Four boards and a passion, no more. There is a cross in the background, used on Sunday, when the nursery kids are taught to pray beneath it. Right now, in front, on stage, a boy and a girl are fondling each other, using two chairs to replace a bed. The boy is long and blond and having a good time, and the girl is short and dark, with good legs, and twitching under his hands. They mumble dialogue into each other's ear and suddenly it is over.

Girls are all about the place. Three or four of them, seated in various parts of the room, poring over scripts. They are auditioning for the part of The Girl In The Bed. They are all colors, from Bronx Black to Ohio Gold. Two earn livings as Laughing Girls on television commercials. The tall, blond boy staggers forward. His name is Karl Schenzer; he is an actor in his late twenties, and he is holding a quart bottle of beer aloft. "Have a drink," he offers, wiping his brow. "How many girls can you take on in an afternoon?"

Come in the evening to Theatre Genesis at St. Mark's and you will see the final product, pure OOB. (There are one-act plays, usually 30 to 45 minutes long, with either the Bed or the Bomb as thematic focus.) The acting is gay and spirited, the dialogue strong and precise. The language down here has no veneer. There is shaping and heightening and general funking, but there is no veneer. It is the pure argot of urban youth. When it hides something it is self-conscious about doing so. In Leonard Melfi's short play *Ferryboat,* recently performed at St. Mark's, the hero erupts after 20 minutes of conversational euphemism and, in a burst of candor, repeatedly using the standard Anglo-Saxon crudity, comes right out and tells her what he wants to do:

> . . . YEAH! How about that now? Do you like that kind of language, huh? Maybe, maybe, I should have just said that to you in the first place, right? I've made a fool of myself, haven't I? Talking and talking a mile a minute. About myself, about everything . . . do you understand?

Divisive words. Just words, but divisive. Those words, for the old church fathers, disfigure everything else St. Mark's does. They've been to a few plays and films. The congregation—old ladies, lawyers, young secretaries, other writers, poets, painters—come and laugh in the right places and applaud and contribute money and then they go home—or to their Bible Study Groups—and argue, trying, like Miss Ethel Berger, to *understand,* in a brisk, businesslike way, just as they try to understand Scripture.

When they argue about the plays the congregation splits into three rigidly defined groups: one in three connects completely. One in three sits right on the fence, hearing the worst of the plays with stoic forbearance. The final third, strengthened by the majority of the Negro middle class, says no, no, no. "I don't see what dirty words teach you," says Mrs. Adelaide Muster, who has been donating volunteer help to St. Mark's for many years. "I'd prefer using that money for other things," says Mrs. Elizabeth Brown, "and not those bearded playwrights. Do you know we spend $10,000 a year on our arts program?"

But listen to the mothers in Bible Study, the ones who sit in the middle. Everyone comes to Bible Study on Tuesday nights: the Rector, the Lay Minister for the Arts, Ralph Cook himself, the vestry, the mothers. They gather in three separate groups, in flats and homes all over the Lower East Side. They talk about the most recent play, *The Box,* by Murray Mednick. It is a wild play, dominated by two lonely, isolated young men who say whatever comes into their lonely, isolated minds for 30 minutes straight. "It was fascinating," says one lady, "but I did get a little tired of that word. I wish these children could forget about all that sex for a while." "My children couldn't understand it," says a young mother, "until I told them it had to do with the bomb."

The Rector, sitting in the living room with them, smiles and harks back to Sam Shepard's play, *The Rock Garden.* It is a play he cherishes and it is easily the most controversial play St. Mark's has yet staged. There are three characters only—a boy and his parents. Until the last few minutes the dialogue is monopolized by the father and the mother, who drone on in complete vacuity, piling inanity upon inanity and wearing the audience's patience thin. Then, suddenly, the boy leaps to his feet and burst forth with a long, lyrical description of the sex act, unrivaled in detail in either Restoration or Roman drama. When he is finished, his father falls off his chair and the play ends. The Rector has written a sermon about this play. He turns now to its theme. "The play is dominated to the end by the parents, whose conversation is filled with subtle sexual imagery, hypocritically disguised. They boy is franker than they are, that's all, and maybe he thinks sex is not evil. I believe this whole generation of young people is saying to us, in effect, 'Look, you use beautiful words and do ugly things; we'll take ugly words and make beauty out of them.' "

The mothers smile. They are not sure they understand and not sure they agree, but they trust him. They have heard him speak, along with the Negro curate Allen Ford, about the necessity to meet people—all kinds of people—*where they are.* But there is more to his motives than that. The young rector is convinced, in a thousand complicated little ways the old church fathers would not understand, that the church does get through to playwrights like Shepard. "They will be, in time, Christian playwrights," he says.

The playwrights, for their part, protest vigorously. "On the contrary," says young Tom Sankey, "we are converting Christianity. Can't you see it happening everywhere? The Catholics have finally absolved the Jews, the theologians admit God Is Dead, the sermons say sex is good. No, we playwrights and artists worship a different God, and the other congregation at St. Mark's is coming over to us, not the reverse."

Leonard Melfi, the most prolific of the playwrights developed by Theatre Genesis, feels the same way. "I've never felt so free in my life as I have writing for St. Mark's. I have a theory, you know, that sexual fantasies are a necessary opiate for the people, so to speak, and most of my plays are sexual fantasies. But the church plays them without a whimper. Oh, you might say that this freedom I've found there has given me a new respect for the church. Yes, you could say that, but no more."

The king of the middle level—and the man who irritates the outside Christians the most—is tall, thin Ralph Cook, who runs the art program as well as directs plays. It is he who makes people like Melfi and Sankey feel at home by rigorously avoiding the merest taints of Christian jargon. "My major job here," he is fond of saying, "is to destroy the church." Words like that are music to the ears of the artistic community. Cook has the face of a beatnik Lincoln, the eyes of a literate Dalmatian. He came wandering in off the street one Sunday, or so legend goes, his life, which included training in the theater, completely disrupted; something about Michael Allen got to him, however, and here he is, back in the bosom of God.

Ralph Cook doesn't say much about God in public, however. Appearing recently on a network television show devoted to drama in the church, he said, in fact, that he personally didn't care whether the actors and playwrights in Theatre Genesis had been baptized at all. The Episcopal Diocese of New York, overhearing, demanded a printed disclaimer be inserted after his portion of the show was concluded. It was.

The artists of the East Village love his Lincoln face and the ascetic jokes and the total artistic freedom he symbolizes. When he was married in the spring they refused to enter the church, of course, but milled about outside in great numbers to salute and later to toast him. He is their Guru, as holy a Guru as they can tolerate. Another way of putting it is the way Arthur Atha, lawyer and senior warden, puts it. "Ralph," he says, "has warmed up a lot of people who might otherwise never step inside a church."

Cook connects with the underground film-makers, too, and they with him. St. Mark's has indeed been at the center of two great artistic renaissances in the East Village, not only Off-Off Broadway, but the

Experimental Film. Today underground films can be seen everywhere, but not long ago the police threatened every public showing. Early last year the church opened its doors for the film-makers and in they came, with loads of neat films, every Monday night, films about politics and colors and sexual organs and bedtime sports and war and nonsense. "The St. Mark's program has been a kind of sanctuary for film-makers," says Bob Cowan, a critic for the *Village Voice* and one of the early organizers of the film program. "We feel we can show anything there and we do."

Sanctuary! For *Scorpio Rising,* for *Green Desire,* for *Alphaville Revisited* or . . . Communism. Yes, sanctuary, the church as a sanctuary for artists. It's happening all over—down in Greenwich Village at Judson Memorial, out in Brooklyn Heights at Spencer Memorial, in cities and suburbs all over the country—this mating of the church and the arts. Spontaneous, spreading, all at once, the church opening up, the artists coming in. As natural as spring. Maybe this is what Dietrich Bonhoeffer meant when he spoke about the future form of religionless Christianity. Maybe he meant this liason between the church and her former enemies.

Why, then, does the marriage seem so noticeable at St. Mark's? Because the church's partner there is the East Village, the center of arts everywhere, the center of the progression forward. They are at the front together, the old church and the young, swinging, scatological Village, shaking and rocking and rattling and changing.

But don't forget The True Believers. They're back at the service, every Sunday. One has to go back there, back to the service, back to the nave and the old, worn pews, back to the bare-headed girls in Levi's and the lean, harried magazine editors and maverick Madison Avenue types and the students who file in at 11 o'clock. Here, by the church's own admission, is its test. WHAT DO THEY BELIEVE? Is God Dead? Is the throne vacant?

The service at St. Mark's is brisk and spirited. It moves quickly. The drama in this part of the church has traditional form and coherence. There is the Old Testament lesson (Isaiah 40:1-11: "All flesh is grass, and all the goodliness thereof is as the flower of the field) and the Holy Communion and the Nicene Creed and finally the sermon. The congregation is hushed and ready. It has sung and read aloud and mumbled and gesticulated, all with pagan zeal. It waits now. The Rector makes his way to the pulpit. He is a solid, definite figure, and his hair, rarely shorn, rises in great manes to either side of the part that divides it. "Mountains and valleys are great, you know," he says, "but you get more speed on the desert. Look at the mountains and the valleys. They are beautiful to look at in their loftiness and depths . . . but progress is slow. It is slow to make your way through the mountains. But you get more speed on the desert. There are no constructions. Nothing, just lots of flat space and room for a highway . . . no loveliness to regard, just flat space and lots of speed."

It is going to be one of his metaphorical sermons. The desert—ugly but better, in the end, than all the grandeur of the highlands. The libido for the ugly, in Christian terms. But it has its application here, in what conventional taste might call an ugly part of the city, in a congregation that smells neither of money nor power, among kids—forsaken? The line is from the Mark of St. Mark's: "God, my God, why hast Thou forsaken me?" and it makes you think of a couple, not far away, a young, white, pregnant unmarried girl and a Negro poet. They have talked about St. Mark's before. "We told the curate of St. Mark's more than we ever told anyone," the girl had said, "even my psychiatrist. He didn't blink an eye. He just asked how could he help. Without St. Mark's we would have missed many a meal." The Poet, too: "We know St. Mark's doesn't condone what we're doing. But it doesn't turn us away, either. If it hadn't been for St. Mark's I suppose I'd be completely estranged from religion now."

"More speed on the desert." It's a metaphor the couple will understand. The Rector returns to it again as his sermon ends. So, soon, will the service. The congregation is on its feet, in fact, responding to the curate, who stands with arms outstretched, flanked on either side by the gold of two crosses and beneath by the starched white of the altar cloth. "Let us bless the Lord," he says. "It is meet and right to do so," the people answer.

The service is over. The True Believers, the inner level at St. Mark's, file out. They don't look like a Rockford, Ill., congregation and they don't talk like one. At the door a film-maker shakes the rector's hand. "I like that image about the desert. And lo, Father, I was turned on."

Do they believe truly? No one knows. It is like the relationship between Batman and Robin, an impassable mystery. One knows only that they are here in the church, now in the Parish Hall, sampling coffee and cake. But that's the point. The banker out in a parish hall in Westchester, mouthing inanities about golf, what does *he* believe? Is one congregation blameless, the other maverick?

The young seminarians from Union love St. Mark's. They come down here and work out their "field" requirements. They are exchanging coffee talk now with the Rector. The pretty young thing from Illinois doesn't connect with *all* of it, to be sure. She is rumored to have walked out on *Alphaville*. But she stays on, thrilled by all the social work and community spirit and intelligent people. "But I don't see," she confides to

Rector Allen, "how all those things can be relative. I mean the films and how they affect the children. You can't be relative about the Ten Commandments, *can* you?"

The Rector munches on his cake. "Linda, things have always been relative. When I was in the Army——"

Gib Turner, another Union Seminarian working at St. Mark's, however, has gotten the news. He turns away from Linda and the poor Rector and his eyes begin to dance. "I came down to St. Mark's to get involved with life," he says. "In fact, that's why I came to Union. Union is mixed up in everything, politics, poverty, civil rights, the arts. That's what we want. I had a Rockefeller grant and could choose my school. I chose Union—and so did 27 of the 50 winners this year."

This is the news. This grasping, greedy, vital need on the part of the young churchmen and the young theologians to get in touch with *life*. You can trace it way back to the beginning of the Death of God movement, back to Dietrich Bonhoeffer, the unfortunate German pastor trapped in a Nazi cell, writing letters to his friend about the coming age of man and what it meant for the future of Christianity:

> God is teaching us that we must live as men who can get along very well without Him. . . . Man must therefore plunge himself into the life of a godless world. . . . He must live a "worldly" life and so participate in the suffering of God. . . . The church stands now where human powers give out, not on the borders, but in the center of the village.

Worldly. That's what the church is about today, about worldliness. No more old lady rectors and old lady masques and old lady parties. Look at Rector Allen, with his pile of Beatle records and his beer and his cigars. Yet, and this is also the news, the worldliness meshes with Bible Study, with Isaiah 40:1-11, with Matthew 18:3.

"A lot of the talk about God Is Dead is silly and hysterical," the Rector says, relaxing at home in his study. "What some of us are saying is that a certain kind of God is dead, the God, you might say, of state religion. It's a subtle matter, just like the presence of dirty words in the church. I'm not afraid of words. The church may be, but I'm not. And the church simply isn't that important. What I'm interested in, what Bonhoeffer was interested in, is the Way, the Christian Way. Christ was no churchman. He was against the church and some of its evils. Hell, yes, the church is in its grave, the church as an instrument of social power, that is. The Way lives on.

"Another thing. I'm not interested in a congregation filled with blameless middle-class people. I care about people who sin boldly. The church's attitude toward such people is to cop out. I'm not going to do that. I do a land-office business in here in unmarried couples, because that's the way the East Village is. It's full of them and they need help badly. I don't approve of many of the things these kids do and write and paint but that doesn't mean I refuse to listen to them."

It's the gait and manner of the man that is important. The old guard doesn't see that. They're irritated subconsciously by the manner, too, but on top they're listening to *what* he says and they are terrified. How many pulpits have lashed out at young men like Robinson and Alitzer as though they were on safari, gun in hand, stalking God?

These young men are changing the rules, not the game. "It matters to be a committed Christian and walk in the world," Michael Allen says, matching conviction with the earliest disciple, "the center of the world, and face it all, all the ugliness and depravity and beauty and conflict with ideas different from your own. There is where I want to be, walking in the center, and not out on the edge someplace, on the border."

The center of the village. That's where the church wants to be, where everything else is, mixing it up with the arts and profanity and politics, taking it all in, gluing all the disparate pieces of our consciousness together, much like Rauschenberg and Johns and other saints. That's what the man meant about the revolution in form. Read St. Mark's in-the-Bouwerie as a work of art, and love it in its new octopus form. Let it alone, too, they say, let it run on a screen somewhere to its heart's content. Underneath, the news is, these young men believe, good, good, good.

The Quest for Community on the Campus

SEYMOUR MARTIN LIPSET
AND
PHILIP G. ALTBACH

American students astonished their elders by their political activism in the Berkeley Revolt of 1964. The language of the present generation of students, as anyone who has taught them knows, is all too often characterized by terms and phrases signifying alienation and the loss of any sense of community cohesion. Thus, to pick at random from the pages of this essay, a sizable proportion, if by no means a majority, of today's students seem to "lack any sense of tradition," are "constantly worrying about their status," feel like "depersonalized IBM cards," and complain of being "alone on a campus of strangers."

Part of the problem seems to be due to the fact that too many faculty members—especially at the high-prestige universities, where publishing is more important than teaching—have lost contact with their students. At the same time, these faculty members have come to mistrust administrators, as well as the government officials and community leaders who sit on boards of trustees and make important decisions which affect their lives. The term "mistrust" surely symbolizes the campus conflicts of today just as it did the class conflicts described in the first two selections. While not offering any simple solutions to these vexing campus problems, this selection explores student attitudes in some detail, and provides considerable insight into the nature and extent of the modern generational conflict, both here in America and in other parts of the world.

Excerpted from "Student Politics and Higher Education in the United States" by Seymour Martin Lipset and Philip G. Altbach, in *Student Politics,* edited by Seymour Martin Lipset, © 1967 by Basic Books, Inc., Publishers, New York.

In recent years, American students, previously noted more for their political apathy than their interest in governmental issues, have received worldwide attention for their political activism in the past year. Starting with the Berkeley "revolt" of 1964, the American campus has seemingly exploded with political and social action, and the "new student left" has become the subject of much analysis—by educators worried about the tranquility of their institutions, government officials concerned about "subversive" influences on the campus, social scientists interested in political movements, and by the mass media. The number of articles, books, and dissertations on the new student movement in the United States has become substantial.

In the past decade, various events have taken place which have emphasized the importance of students in politics and higher education in many of the developing areas. Spurred by student demonstrations which have succeeded in toppling governments in such nations as Turkey, South Korea, and South Vietnam, both academic observers and government officials have taken an increased interest in student political activities and movements. The historical role of students in various independence movements, in India, Burma, Vietnam, Algeria, and other nations, and their potential as "incipient elites" in many new nations have also come under analysis. In Spain and Portugal, students have played a major role in demanding more academic and political freedom. More recently, students in the industrially advanced nations have also taken a politically active role, and have obtained their share of newspaper headlines. Student strikes in France, Italy, and West Germany demanding better educational facilities, and the recent upsurge of American student activity seem to indicate a new political consciousness on the part of students.

This [article] will examine the American student movement in an effort to analyze some of the causes and effects of student political involvement in the United States, and to link this activity to trends in the developing nations. We are convinced that students are, in certain circumstances, an important political element, and that, in any case, political activity is often a vital means of socialization for students. In many nations where the student population is small and mostly composed of the offspring of the various elites, student activism has been of crucial importance in national politics.

At the outset, it should be made clear that we recognize that the scope of the American student "revolution" has been greatly exaggerated by the mass media, which have seized upon dramatic forms of student political activity and have devoted substantial attention to them. Student political organizations involve only a tiny minority of the total student population in the United States. The *National Guardian,* a left-wing newspaper, has estimated that there are perhaps 12,000 members of *all* of the various "new left" organizations in the United States, with a similar number of sympathizers. Representatives of the "new left" Students for Democratic Society claim 20,000 members and supporters. When it is remembered that there are about 6,000,000 students in American colleges and universities, this figure is not very significant. Most American institutions of higher education have not been affected by the "new left." A comprehensive study of student activism during 1964–65, based on replies to questionnaires from the deans of students in 849 institutions, reports the total absence of student radicals in 74 per cent of them. In the remaining group, those who filled out the questionnaires checked the lowest possible category of response other than "none," i.e., "less than 5 per cent," in all but .5 per cent of the cases. Student leftism, involvement in civil rights activities, and opposition to the Vietnamese war, are largely associated with size and quality of university. The smaller private and denominational colleges, many state universities, and almost all technological schools have seen no demonstrations, have no chapters of left-wing or civil rights groups, and their student bodies do not exhibit much political awareness.

. . .

VARIATIONS IN SUPPORT: THE MOOD OF THE FACULTY

The support for more radical student political actions may be analyzed in terms of types of institutions in which such activity is more common, and of the traits which characterize the individuals who participate. On the whole, as we have noted, radical student political activity has been limited to a relatively small number of colleges and universities, predominantly large schools with good faculties (as indicated by proportions with Ph.D's among them). Three universities appear to stand out as centers of organized student activity in recent years. These are the University of California at Berkeley, the University of Michigan (Ann Arbor), and the University of Wisconsin (Madison). These three institutions are the leading state universities as judged by national rankings of faculty scholarly eminence, are quite big (close to 30,000 students each), have a very large graduate student enrollment including many who remain around campus for many years, are located at some considerable distance from the national centers of political power and influence, and have a largely non-local student body. Sheer numbers mean that a relatively small percentage of the total student population can mount a large demonstration. (For example, the sit-in at Sproul Hall, the administration building, which was the high point of the Berkeley revolt, involved close to 700 students or less than 3 per cent of the student body.)

Since other equally large state universities—if less eminent from the scholarly point of view—have originated less potent political protest, some have argued that the tensions reflected at these three institutions arise in part from aggrieved faculty members, whose conditions of work and sense of a lack of proper intellectual style create resentment against both the university and the larger society and polity. Berkeley, of course, stands in a class by itself since the two largest and most noteworthy campus protests in a 15-year period both occurred there, the fight against the non-Communist Loyalty Oath in 1949–1950, and the Free Speech controversy in 1964–1965. While both of these conflicts were initiated by stupid, reactionary, and restrictive changes by the Regents or administration, these precipitating events cannot be regarded as the primary "causes." One can point to comparable attacks on academic and political freedom at many other large state universities and at some distinguished private ones which did not result in comparable faculty reactions. Clearly, the Berkeley social system has been more unstable than those of other institutions. As the most successful "upwardly mobile" institution in American academe, it has endured many of the tensions of growth and development comparable to those faced by the state of California generally. And it may be suggested that just as the latter facilitate larger extremist movements of the left and right in the state, the exacerbation of social relations among faculty, students and administration, inherent in the successful pursuit of academic eminence, has contributed to making possible the considerable political unrest and attacks against the university from within.

As most discussions of sources of student unrest have ignored the possibility that student attitudes reflect the mood of significant sections of the faculty, we would like to first discuss faculty dissatisfactions at the prestigious state universities. It is difficult to pinpoint the sources of these resentments, but some of them would seem to reflect institutional and personal status insecurities. These schools, though having large numbers of distinguished faculty, lack the sense of permanent traditional eminence which is possessed by the old private universities of the East. In a sense, the major public universities resemble in their position and behavior, the *nouveaux riches,* who constantly worry about their status and who seek evidence that they have really arrived. The more ancient prestigeful schools, like aristocratic old families, can ignore external opinion. The insecurity of these state universities is directly reflected in their lesser willingness to appoint their own graduates to faculty positions; they would rather rely on the judgment of others. It also shows up in the greater concern evidenced for the national rankings of departments, and for the number of awards achieved by faculty. This institutional concern results in an internal salary and reward structure which is largely geared to the market; invidious salary differentials of large magnitudes become a mechanism to recruit and retain eminent or highly promising scholarly "productive" faculty. And these differentials, in turn, create considerable resentments among faculty toward the institution.

Intellectual life is inherently very competitive, but the structure and values of the distinguished public universities magnify the factors making for competitive resentments, while some of the older major private universities are able to follow policies which somewhat reduce these pressures through the fact that they can rely on institutional prestige to secure and hold faculty, many of whom are their own former students. As one Yale professor who had also taught at Berkeley put it, an Ivy League professor is much less likely to find himself "trumped" by a younger man than he would be at Berkeley. At less distinguished and less ambitious public institutions, administration and faculty aspirations are presumably lower, and consequently there is less pressure for invidious internal differentiation, and less resentment at institutional failings. The significant difference is not whether an institution is public or private, but whether it aspires to academic eminence, and can or can not rely on ascriptive prestige. Thus a private school which appears to fall into the same category as the big three of the state universities, Brandeis University, seems to have many of the internal problems and faculty political resentments found at Madison or Berkeley. The University of Chicago, which has been in the forefront of private university student protest in 1966, also has been characterized by a sharply invidious internal reward system. Whether consequent strains help account for the faculty minority which encouraged on-campus civil disobedience is not known. Unlike Berkeley, a large majority of the Chicago faculty strongly backed the administration's refusal to negotiate while under pressure.

Institutional differences between public and private universities can, however, play an important role in determining the professional self-image, attitudes, and performance of the faculty. Public institutions are intrinsically under greater external pressures than their private counterparts. Dependent on public authorities for a large proportion of their budgets, and under the often careful scrutiny of legislators, journalists, and others who feel that the state university is within their domain of competence, these institutions must always be on their guard against outside political and other pressures. This fact has acted in subtle ways to diminish the status and security of the faculty, as well as to make administrations more careful in their actions. Interference with largely academic matters by publicly appointed or elected university trustees, who are necessarily more involved in their own non-academic concerns than in higher education, has had bad effects at Berkeley, and is an important problem for many state universities. In contrast, the major private institutions have few such worries. Their presidents usually have only to report to distinguished trustees, who are almost invariably alumni, and who see one of their main roles as the defense of the university from outside pressure. It is, after all, much easier to appeal to the institutional loyalties of the alumni than it is to the state legislature.

The fact that state university professors are often made aware of substantial outside control encourages the feeling among them that they are not "trusted" to make their own decisions, thus creating a sense of low status. The faculty is affected in more subtle ways by public scrutiny. Faculty members are encouraged by the administration and senior colleagues to impose a kind of self-censorship on their activities or statements for fear of public condemnation of the university. This vulnerability of public universities to outside pressure and scrutiny has had some important effects on faculty and administration. In an effort to protect their academic independence and freedom, public university faculties have attempted to achieve the maximum degree of academic self-government. Decisions which at first-rate private institutions are usually made by administrators must be dealt with by faculty committees at major public universities. This proliferation of committees has meant that professors at California, Wisconsin, and Michigan spend a good deal more time in meetings of various kinds than do their compeers at Harvard, Yale, and Princeton. It has also increased the potential for intra-faculty factionalism and dispute, since professors at the more "democratic" institutions are more likely to blame each other for unpopular decisions. A common complaint at public institutions is the large amount of time taken up in committee meetings. At the University of California, one of the explicit criteria for faculty advancement is "service to the university," which usually means participation in various committees. The system is institutionalized to this extent.

Elaborate mechanisms of academic self-government may provide the faculty with the institutionalized means of resisting high authority in periods of crisis. They also, however, make for institutional conservatism, since, as Martin Trow suggests, "Deans are usually more hospitable to experiments and innovations than are faculty committees." And administrators in academic polities which involve considerable consultation with such committees tend to be weak, chosen for their ability to get along, rather than for their scholarly eminence or leadership qualities. Ironically, the very faculty which demand as much self government as possible often bitterly criticize their administrators for lack of leadership abilities, lack of foresight in anticipating problems, and inability to cope with external pressures, liabilities which are inherent in the weakness of the role.

The greater size of the faculty and student body at the major public institutions compared to the private schools creates other frustrations and tensions. With larger departments and faculties, more meetings become necessary and more formal rules must be imposed. And in accordance to some Parkinson's law, these factors tend to create more factionalism, to limit the freedom of the individual professor to pursue his own interests without interference from others. . . .

The differences between the elite private schools and the best state institutions which affect the attitude of the faculty to the university and polity are not solely a consequence of the strains of achieved as compared to the security of ascribed institutional status, or to differences which may be attributed to variations in size or type of external control. Variations in the quality of the student body are also relevant. Even the best state institutions have a student body which is quite heterogeneous in intellectual quality as compared with a rather consistent high level in the top private schools.[1] Although concern for research and other forms of intellectually creative activities is great among the faculties at all major universities, whether public or private, it seems evident that those at the elite private institutions take their teaching activities much more seriously, secure more intrinsic rewards from feeling that they are good

[1] The heterogeneity of large public universities has been graphically documented by Martin Trow. Among the 5,000 freshmen who enter Berkeley each year, one-quarter could not name the Secretary of State, and half had never read a book of poetry for pleasure. By contrast, 90 per cent of the freshmen entering three selective liberal arts colleges could name the Secretary of State, and three-quarters had read poetry for pleasure. Half the freshmen at the university owned more than fifteen books, while 70–80 per cent did at the three colleges. The results of the Scholastic Aptitude Tests (SAT) tend to corroborate these findings. At Harvard, M.I.T., Stanford, and Cal Tech "between 70 and 90 per cent of their entering freshmen had SAT Verbal scores of over 600. At Berkeley the comparable figure was 30 per cent." At the private universities, no more than 21 per cent had scores lower than 500, while at Berkeley one-third scored below 500—this despite the fact that Berkeley is one of the most selective state universities. "In 1960 Berkeley admitted . . . 420 students with SAT Verbal scores of over 650, and almost a thousand with SAT scores of over 600, more at that level than enter M.I.T. and Amherst combined." Berkeley also admitted 1,500 students with scores below 500—more than triple the number with scores that low who were admitted to Kutztown State College in Pennsylvania.

teachers, than do those at the big three of the state schools. In a recent article on American students, Martin Meyerson, former Acting Chancellor at Berkeley, who taught for many years at Harvard, eloquently summed up some of the sources of these distinctions.

> At Oxford and Cambridge, Harvard, Yale, and Princeton, the rewards of teaching included the faculty's sense—even if not articulated—that their students were the sons of the famous or were themselves apt to be famous in the future. It is more attractive for teachers to spend time with the well-prepared and potentially powerful, than with the mediocre student of humble origins. The professor's frequent preference is to devote intellectual and leisure energies to colleagues or in some cases to men of affairs; he can be motivated to attention toward his students by a sense of duty, but this sense functions best when duty is reinforced by pleasure. And the pleasure the teacher gets seems to increase with the intellectual and social standing of his pupils.

These factors encourage the active and distinguished scholars at the major private institutions to devote greater energies to teaching, and also give to those who are less competent and unrecognized as scholars a greater sense of achievement, of satisfaction with their jobs as teachers, than their equivalents spend or secure at comparably eminent public institutions. This assumption concerning the lesser commitment to teaching of faculty at major public universities is reflected in the opinions of the faculty themselves.

> When a sample of Berkeley faculty was asked recently, "What proportion of the faculty members here would you say are strongly interested in the academic problems of students?" only a third answered "almost all" or "over half," as compared with 85–90 per cent giving those responses among the faculty at three selective liberal arts colleges. The faculty's judgments of their colleagues is closely reflected in their students' judgment of them.

These comments on the institutional variations between the leading public and private universities, which adversely affect faculty morale and values at the better public institutions assume that faculty attitudes and behavior are a major source of influence on the political stance of students. At both Berkeley and Michigan, members of the faculty have shown a willingness to attack the university as a means of attaining political ends in ways that would be unthinkable at the older major private universities.

VARIATIONS IN SUPPORT: STUDENT REACTIONS

The thesis that heterogeneity and size contribute to discontent may also be argued on the student level. The three major state schools recruit an intellectually much abler student body, particularly for their massive graduate student programs, than do the other public universities; yet they have many more students per faculty member than the high ranking private schools. The difference in favor of the prestige private universities would increase greatly if one computed the student to distinguished faculty ratio. A recent survey of Wisconsin student opinion found that 80 per cent felt that the institution is "depersonalized." Over half of the students (59 per cent) expressed agreement with the statement that "Generally speaking, students in today's large university are no longer treated as individuals; instead they have become IBM cards, numbers, cogs in a sort of educational factory." Similiar attitudes have been expressed by Berkeley students in a number of different survey studies. That this type of frustration is specific to the large public universities, and not to college life generally, may be seen from the results of a 1966 national survey of freshmen across the country conducted by the American Council of Education. Forty per cent of the first-year students at public universities expressed agreement with the statement that students at their school are like numbers in a book. The corresponding percentage for private universities was 20, while only 6 per cent of freshmen at four-year private nonsectarian colleges felt the same way. Reliable statistical data indicate a very high drop-out rate among undergraduates in the three high ranking public institutions (50 per cent of those who enter Berkeley as freshmen *do not* graduate. Less than five per cent of those who enter Harvard fail to graduate; the corresponding figure for Stanford across the Bay from Berkeley is under 10 per cent.) The success record among graduate students is also poor.[2] Those who secure their doctorates there, particularly in the social sciences, often take close to a decade to do so. The figures at the major private schools are clearly better on both the graduate and undergraduate levels. The complexity of the large public institutions gives rise to substantial frustrations, among both students and faculty. It is not surprising there seems

[2] A report indicating the varying degrees of success of graduate students in different departments of sociology attests to the sharp variations at the Big Three of the Ivy League and the State Universities in educational achievement. In the academic year 1964–5, Berkeley had more graduate students than any other department in its field, 193, yet reported only 45 completed Ph.D.'s in the preceding nine years. Harvard, on the other hand, has 73 graduate students, but had turned out 86 Ph.D.'s in the same period of time. Similar relative differences exist between Michigan and Wisconsin, on the one hand, and Princeton and Yale on the other.

to be social and political alienation among a significant and often most capable minority within them.

The major state universities remain extremely heterogeneous in their student bodies, not only in terms of intellectual calibre, discussed above, but also in student sub-cultures; they still include large numbers involved in the so-called "collegiate," or fraternity—athletic—social culture; many who are narrowly vocationally oriented, viewing the university solely as a means to attaining a well-paying job; the academically-intellectually inclined; and the "non-conformists." The best private schools, on the other hand, have become increasingly *homogeneous* in the calibre and traits of their students. As Martin Trow has put it:

> In liberal arts colleges and leading private universities, the enormous growth in demand for college places since World War II and the increased selectivity which this has allowed has led to . . . a predominance of able, academically oriented students, the great majority of whom are going on to graduate and professional school, with even their "non-conformists'" and political activists more cautious, more aware of what they have to lose.

The best public institutions are large and attractive enough to support a "non-conformist" sub-culture which is sufficiently large in absolute terms to ignore social or intellectual pressures from the more purely "academic" or "collegiate" sub-cultures. The fact that they are not commuter institutions, that the great majority of their students come from outside the area also contributes to their ability to sustain a "non-conformist" culture. Various studies of student leftists, drug-users, and academically competent "drop-outs" agree that these groups draw heavily from students who are living away from home in off-campus housing, i.e., not in dormitories, houses, or fraternities. The distinguished private schools are also not commuter institutions, but almost all their undergraduates live in university housing and are necessarily involved in a primarily university environment.

Another group of large public universities, those which are located in urban centers, and draw from a less well-to-do student body which lives at home, tend to be much more vocationally oriented, and hence are less supportive of political or social non-conformism. Institutions such as the colleges of the City University of New York, Wayne State University in Detroit, or the various affiliates of Rutgers University in urban New Jersey, were major strongholds of political protest during the 1930's when many of their students feared a lack of opportunity as a result of the Depression. Today, however, upwardly mobile students from less privileged backgrounds can anticipate economically rewarding positions upon graduation. Institutions characterized by large numbers of such students tend to be relatively politically quiescent. (One seeming exception is composed of urban schools with a majority of Jewish students who are disproportionately liberal and left for other reasons.)

The best private institutions, on the other hand, possess a student body which is predominantly academic and intellectual in orientation and which works hard to accomplish the goal of an academic or other type of intellectual career. Such students are usually quite liberal in their political outlook, and are sympathetic to many of the objectives of the student activists. The overwhelming majority of them desist, however, from participation in the more militant activities of the student movement, if for no other reason than they do not have the time to engage in politics and also secure the grades necessary to get into a good graduate school.

The increasing number of graduate students, particularly in the large state universities, provides a major source of encouragement, and more important, continuity in leadership for the activist student movement. There are currently over 500,000 graduate students in the United States. Graduate students, in general, resemble the more academically oriented undergraduates in their political behavior. Although they are relatively sympathetic to activist causes, they are disinclined to participate, given their commitment to scholarship and their clear-cut career orientations. Since many of them are "teaching assistants" in close contact with lower-division under-graduates, they are in a position to communicate the sense of grievance which many of them have to lower-division students who, less involved in scholarship and careerist activities, are freer to act. As Kenneth Keniston has pointed out: "[T]he plight of the graduate student is probably more dire than that of any other student group. . . . The graduate student . . . is often pressured, judged, graded, indentured and exploited." Teaching assistants are obligated to devote a considerable amount of time to teaching (for only a small stipend), while at the same time they must demonstrate their competence as scholars. Graduate students in the liberal arts field are in an especially tension-ridden situation, since their research-minded professors are constantly on the outlook for brilliance. They give their graduate students the sense that they are constantly being judged for their scholarly potential by criteria which are often imprecise and highly subjective. To view the larger society as a competitive "rat race" is but to project the situation of many graduate students onto the total system. Many "drop out" for shorter or longer periods to escape these pressures, while often continuing to live near the campus. Some become available to serve as the "non-student" leaders of campus protest. In groups like SDS, many of the senior leaders, who provide the ideological flavor of the organization, are present or former graduate students. A number of the major figures in the various forms of protest at Berkeley fall in these categories.

If we turn to an examination of the traits which seem to differentiate those who support the new student activism, it may be worth while to examine the assumption that the movement represents an expression of generational conflict, in which those who seek to separate themselves from their conservative elders move to the left for shock effect. Studies of the backgrounds of activists indicate that the opposite, if anything, is true. They are much more often students who are acting out in practice the values which they have been taught by ideologically liberal parents. . . . the study of civil rights activists in SCOPE indicates that they were *not* "rebelling against parental wishes in becoming civil rights participants. Almost two-thirds reported that their parents supported their work in the summer program. About one-half felt that their participation would actually enhance their relationship with their parents . . . only five per cent of the volunteers reported that they didn't get along with or were hostile toward their parents." Almost identical conclusions have been reached by Keniston after examining the results of various studies:

> Indeed, if there is any single psychological thread that runs through student activism today, it is this "identification with parental values." When there is a conflict between parents and their activist offspring, it is usually not over principle but over practice; and when these students criticize their parents, it is not for what their parents believe, but for their failure to practice the beliefs they drummed into their children's ears from an early age. . . . [Most of the activists] . . . get along moderately well with their parents, and most of their parents feel compelled—at least in principle—to support their children's activism.

It is worth noting also that some statistical evidence suggests that a visible number are the children of former radicals. Samuel Lubell reports that those "with radical family upbringing represent a sixth of all the leftists who turned up in my random sample." He comments that "the sons and daughters of one-time Socialists, Communists and other leftists . . . provide the organizing leadership for demonstrations at many campuses." This is not as surprising as it first appears. The Communist Party of the U.S. had about 100,000 members between the mid-1930's and the early 1940's. It also had, according to former leaders, an annual turnover of close to 90 per cent. Consequently the number of former American Communists, many of whom are currently middle class or higher, is well over 500,000. Former participants in the American Socialist Party, and the larger number of "splinter" radical groups add to this number, as do the many "fellow travelers" of both the Communists and Socialists. Many of these people, particularly the former Communists, appear to carry an internal stigma; they fear exposure and have remained on the left in many of their opinions. Moreover, they often feel guilty about their political inactivity and retain a sense of alienation from the mainstream of society. Although now outside of the radical movement, many of them have repeatedly impressed their children with the evils of American society, which they see as denying them some part of their rights as citizens.

The issue of past radical politics apart, a variety of studies suggest that the modal family background characteristics of student activists are intellectually oriented, relatively well-to-do homes, where the "parents maintain a libertarian viewpoint in matters of politics, human relations, and religion . . . [rather than] from the economic and socially deprived. . . ."

. . .

Given the seeming linkage between parental higher (post-graduate) education and political liberalism among parents of university students, it may seem logical therefore, that various researchers also conclude that "intellectualism" and high academic aptitude are also characteristics of this student group. Studies in various emerging nations reported by Metta Spencer and Glaucio Soares also find that those who are favorably disposed toward an "intellectual" rather than a professional or vocational academic style are more likely to "devote great energy to political and social causes." Lubell indicates that among every ten American radical students whom he interviewed "four thought they would like to teach at the college level; two wanted to work as psychologists, one as a journalist or artist, while three were undecided what to do." . . . Those inclined toward the vocational and professional world tend to come from lower socioeconomic or ethnic backgrounds, or from conservative business-managerial families. Lower status origins are conducive to concentration on upward mobility, which many of the activists regard as careerism. Both low status and conservative well-to-do family environments are associated with relative disinterest in politics or with support of right-wing politics.

A somewhat different linkage between personal experiences and student activism may be found in the hypothesis which suggests that students as a stratum are disproportionately drawn to such movements because a campus population inherently contains a large number of socially dislocated individuals, those who have shifted from one social environment to another, and are consequently predisposed to find new values and possibly commit themselves to activism. Berkeley data again are relevant. The faculty Select Committee on Education stressed this factor as contributing to unrest. They point to the large number of Berkeley students who normally drop out and are replaced by transfers, as undermining the potential for a "community." As they comment, "it is hardly surprising that many students feel alone in a community of strangers. In the April 1965 survey, almost two-thirds of the students felt the University to be an 'impersonal institution. . . .'" The study of the police car demonstrators reports that, as a group, they had spent much less time as students at Berkeley than the student body as a whole. A second survey of a sample of those arrested in December 1964 for sitting in at Sproul Hall yielded similar results. This study found that half of the undergraduates arrested were transfer students, many from out of state, i. e., had not begun their college careers at Berkeley or in California. Among the leaders of the FSM, "transfer students were in evidence in significantly larger numbers." More recently, reports on the Spring 1966 anti-draft sit-in at the University of Wisconsin indicate that the three leaders of the demonstration came from metropolitan New York.

There are many factors which seem to correlate with liberal attitudes and support of activism among American university students. While student activists are more irreligious than the campus population as a whole, certain religious backgrounds, mainly Jewish and liberal Protestant, tend to produce a large proportion of them. . . .

Within the university, social science and humanities majors seem to be much more involved in the student movement than those in other fields. A comparison of those who participated in a peace demonstration in Washington compared with "counterpickets" representing student conservative groups indicates clearly the relevant patterns found in a number of studies:

> Of those who gave answers to questionnaire items pertaining to academic vocational areas, two-thirds (66 per cent) were majoring in the humanities or social sciences, with relatively few in the physical or biological sciences, and very few in pre-professional courses. . . . Career plans were often indefinite and were predominantly centered in teaching, social service, and research. This finding stands in marked contrast to the career goals of the "counterpickets" from student conservative groups. These young people were typically very definite about careers in business or law, and were taking appropriate pre-professional courses.

The data linking subject studied in university with political values and activity correspond generally with the information available concerning the politics of university faculties and intellectuals generally. Presumably students in humanistic and social science courses are exposed to more liberalizing and politically activating experiences than those in other fields. Some evidence, however, suggests that the correlations between subjects studied and political beliefs may be more a consequence of self-selection of certain fields by students who are already liberals or conservatives, rather than of influence from their education as such. Thus in one panel (repeat interview) study of student attitudes, Morris Rosenberg found that among freshmen, conservative students were more inclined than others to study business, a not unexpected finding although some nonconservatives made the same choice. When the same students were canvassed two years later, it turned out that their original political beliefs were a good predictor of which students would change their career orientation. The more liberal among those who had initially chosen to be businessmen changed to another career, while the bulk of more conservative business majors remained faithful to their original objective. Further evidence suggesting that the correlation between beliefs and major subject is a product of student selection rather than accumulated learning may be found in a Berkeley study of entering freshmen in 1959 which "showed a distinct correlation between their attitudes and their intended majors, especially among men. The men students who most frequently gave answers indicating their opposition to existing social and political conditions were those entering the humanities and fine arts. The groups which found existing conditions most acceptable were the potential engineers." Lubell reports that students who "plan to go into the professions, business, engineering or the sciences range from 70 to 90 per cent "in favor of the Vietnam war," while "among students who talk of teaching . . . only 47 per cent support the war."

While a clear-cut pattern seems to exist between various background factors, liberal social and political attitudes, and involvement in student activism, it is important to note that these relationships, particularly as they relate to activism, lack certain important comparisons with other types of students. As Barry Metzger points out, while "it appears evident that the radical minority is more middle class, more concentrated in the study of the humanities and social sciences, and more academically distinguished than the campus majority . . . , these generalizations might also be true of *non-radical student activists.*" And the two available studies of the leaders in student government and campus service activities generally indicate that they also differ from the student population at large along the same dimensions as the radical activists. The most comprehensive report on the characteristics of student government leaders, based on a questionnaire survey at the 1966 National Congress of the United States National Student Association, indicates that this group of student "activists," one-third of whom voted for a YAF leader as their next president, tended to resemble those involved in various campus demonstrations, or in organizations like SDS. As contrasted with a national sample of student population generally, the NSA delegates were disproportionately from large metropolitan centers, from relatively well-to-do families, from highly educated backgrounds (26 per cent of their fathers had attended graduate school as compared with the national average of 14 per cent), from families of Eastern European and Jewish origin, majors in the social sciences (51 per cent among the delegates as compared to 11 per cent nationally) or the humanities and arts (21 per cent as compared to 16), and had a history of high scholarly achievement in high school and college.

When we compare students active in conservative groups or demonstrations with those participating in left-wing causes, certain clear differences emerge. The conservatives, on the whole, seem to come from relatively poorer, less educated, more provincial, more Anglo-Saxon, and more Protestant backgrounds than the more liberal activists. And while a study of conservative counter-demonstrators during a Washington peace march found that they came largely from pre-professional, engineering, and business students, the most comprehensive survey of the members and leaders of campus conservative clubs in a large number of universities reported that they resembled the leftists in their college major. Almost half of them (47 per cent) were majoring in the social sciences, with another 18 per cent in the humanities, much like the student government and liberal social-action group participants. The comparative analysis of SDS and YAF convention delegates also reported that social-science majors were overrepresented in both groups (63 per cent in SDS and 45 per cent in YAF).

Most surprising of all the recent research on American student attitudes and behavior are the findings of Dr. Joseph Katz of Stanford University, who reports that a comprehensive, continuous long-term study of samples of the Berkeley and Stanford student bodies indicates that a considerable majority at each school is passive and conformist:

> When we asked these students what they expected to be doing ten years from now, they often replied with a description of a suburban existence that they considered rather routine. . . . Our questionnaire and interview data confirm for more than the majority of students a strongly "privatist" orientation. They rank highest their own individual careers and future family life. Involvement in international, national or civic affairs, helping other people, are ranked astonishingly low and there is little change from the freshman to the senior year.

The conclusions reached by Katz in his Berkeley-Stanford study coincide with those derived from an examination of surveys in different parts of the country. Kenneth Keniston also reports that "a vast majority of American students remains privatistic. There are various reasons for this emphasis on private individual goals, but not the least of which is the enormous increase in pressure to attain good grades which increasingly has been placed on American students, in high school, college, and graduate school. The combination of the demands to upgrade the level of American education which followed as a reaction to the Russian lead in space science (the post-Sputnik craze), and the effects of greater numbers pressing for entrance to good universities and graduate schools than there are places, even for excellent students, has changed the quality of education. Students are now pressed by their parents and teachers as no other generation in American history has ever been pushed. To relax while in school may lead to disaster. In seeking to explain the seriousness, the inability to relax, which has been attributed to many students, the philosopher Charles Frankel points out: "The students have been on a treadmill for a long long time. There are the pressures of college boards, pressures of parents, pressures of the competition for grades."

In a real sense, American students have been placed in a situation comparable to that long faced by Japanese teen-agers. In Japan, there is enormous pressure to work hard to prepare for the intensely competitive examinations for college entrance. A variety of novels and studies have pointed to the way in which this pressure upsets Japanese youngsters. And two of the consequences which are reputed to flow from this pressure are the high suicide rate among teen-agers, and the often rather militant and ultra-radical political activities of Japanese college students. Studies of Japanese student politics indicate that much of the well-publicized activism is the work of freshmen and sophomores who are able to relax upon entering the university, since Japanese universities give only infrequent examinations, and traditionally grade easily.

Those who are admitted do not have to work hard. Political activity drops off as they approach graduation and face a new set of competitive examinations to qualify for good posts in industry or government. One may point to similar reactions in the United States. The suicide rate among young people of high school and college age has risen rapidly while that of older age cohorts has been declining. A comparison of rates in 1950–1952 with those a decade later reveals a total increase of 4 per cent among all white American males. The suicide rate, however, jumped *48 per cent* among the 15–19 age category, and 26 per cent among those in the 20–24-years-old group. It actually *fell* for men 55 years and older . . .

Studies of student politics suggest that while a higher proportion of more advanced and graduate students have liberal and radical attitudes than do those in lower division classes, the freshmen and sophomores are more likely to show higher rates of participation in demonstrations. Thus a study of a Washington peace demonstration indicates that "30 per cent were college freshmen, 15 per cent were sophomores, 15 per cent juniors, and 11 per cent were seniors. Only 6 per cent identified themselves as graduate students in a university. . . . The mean age of the demonstrators was 18½, with *45 per cent of the sample being either 18 or 19 years of age.* Twenty per cent were 17 and under." Similar findings were reported in a study of a militant Washington, D.C., student civil rights group. At Berkeley, also, freshmen and sophomores were the most over-represented classes among those arrested in Sproul Hall, while graduate students, the most ideologically liberal group in the school, were by far the most under-represented in the sit-in. Over one-third of the student body is graduate, but only 19 per cent of those arrested fell in this category.

These findings concerning the greater propensity of freshmen to engage in political activism may tie in with the findings of psychological research that "the freshman year is a particularly stressful one. . . . [F]or entering freshmen the sudden impact of academic requirements, homesickness, new living arrangements and peers constitute especially unsettling conditions." Participation in group activity in a conflict situation may give the insecure and lonely freshman that sense of identity and involvement which he lost when leaving home and high school.

We would suggest that the willingness to break loose against authority afforded by activism, the growth in the use of drugs, and the increase in drop-outs by able students, as well as the emphasis on privatism and self-orientation reported by Katz and Keniston, are to some considerable degree a reaction to the competitive stresses placed on today's students. They are under extreme coercion, and it is not surprising that some, from extremely privileged backgrounds, strike out against the system, that they see the university as an agency of authority which fosters the "rat race," that they welcome an opportunity to secede, to get off the treadmill. But though a small minority take the activist or secessionist responses, the great majority accept their role and conform, though they may want to do other things. . . .

The evidence presented here that the vast majority of American students are privatistic, careerist, and moderate in their politics does not mean that the university is a conservative environment. Some schools are, of course, but the majority of universities do seem to have a liberalizing effect on a large number of their students with regard to their attitudes to civil rights, religion, and domestic politics.

But though the campus seems to be a liberalizing place for some students, it is characterized generally by the values and attitudes of the educated middle classes. Students, on the average, are somewhat more liberal than their parents. Their attitudes on issues such as civil rights, welfare state legislation, government economic planning, or the propensity to vote Democratic are more liberal than the mainstream of the middle class, particularly since 1960. Recent events in American student political life have shown that it is possible to remove students from their liberal but generally apathetic tendencies during a crisis. When the chips are down, as they were in Berkeley, a large proportion of the students supported the militants of the Free Speech Movement, even though the overwhelming majority did not normally take part in politics, and have not remained active in the student movement. Similarly, such students will back a movement for civil rights in the campus community.

When one considers American students on the scale of conventional radicalism, those who attend the universities in the United States must be considered a fairly conservative and passive community. The tiny handful who make up the attention-getting "new left" apart, one must agree with the conclusion of Joseph Katz concerning the vast majority, that "the primary need still is to wake up students, not to constrain them."

Despite the fact that the proportion of students in the United States who are alienated from the values of the mainstream of society and who are active in politics is very small, this minority has been able to achieve notable successes. The fact that a small proportion of the student body at Berkeley could arouse the sympathy of large numbers of students, and that groups like the SDS can have so widespread an influence on the campus (even if their influence is much less than what the mass media would have us believe) is very significant. The reasons for this phenomenon are not difficult to discern. The very political vacuum on the campus makes it easier for a minority to be heard and for it to exercise an influence far beyond its numbers. A study by Glaucio Soares dealing with students in many countries indicates that even where student political activity is highly institutionalized, the numbers of those actively involved are relatively small. The ideologically committed students (of either right or left, although predominantly the left) are able to dominate university politics because of their higher degree of political commitment and level of activity. A survey of the attitudes of Japanese students toward the militant Zengakuren-led demonstrations against the U.S.–Japan Security Treaty in 1960 showed that 60 per cent of the students thought that the activities of the Zengakuren were "too radical" while only 10 per cent felt that they were proper. The Zengakuren, however, was able to effectively control the student movement, and to lead it for an extended period in extremely militant political activity. President Eisenhower cancelled his visit to Japan, and the Kishi government ultimately fell largely because of the activity of this militant student minority. When the heat of the political crisis was ended, however, many of the students who had been involved in the movement returned to their classes, and did not continue to take part in the student movement.

The majority of moderate students everywhere are not only generally less concerned with politics, expressing interest in social or cultural activity and in their own careers, but when they do have political interests, their commitment tends to be weaker than that of the radicals. Thus, moderates will act less decisively on issues, and will be less concerned with politics in any case.

The ability of American student activists to mobilize a visible base of demonstrators on large campuses from a national student population of close to six millions should not be confused with the revolt of the students as a stratum. It is probably true that, in absolute numbers, more students are involved in protest activity than at any time since the World War II (although it should be recalled that the pre-war student movement was numerically larger than the present movement, and that in terms of the proportion of involved students to the total student population, it was vastly more significant). On the other hand, there seems to be little doubt that only a small fraction of the total student population is so engaged, and that the number of students who consider themselves politically aware is also small. This small fraction has the passive support of most students when it is pressing for civil rights or academic freedom. But its support dwindles when it demonstrates against American foreign policy or for a specific ideological program.

THE AMERICAN STUDENT MOVEMENT AND THE DEVELOPING AREAS: SOME COMPARATIVE COMMENTS

The recent attention given both to student activities in the United States and to student unrest in many of the developing areas makes some comparative discussion both relevant and feasible. These comments are necessarily incomplete, and are only intended to underline some of the more obvious factors which we have observed.

American student politics, like American politics generally, tends to be rather pragmatic and non-ideological in its approach. No directly left-wing party-related student organization in the United States has ever achieved a mass following. The only groups which have made a strong impact on the student population have been those concerned with a specific issue, such as civil rights, or more broadly based social action groups, such as Students for a Democratic Society, at present, or the American Student Union during the 1930's. Political ideologies still have an important attraction, particularly to students in many of the developing nations, and are often the base of substantial student movements. The fact that student groups are able to fall back on ideology—usually some form of Marxism—makes it easier for such groups to survive periods of political quiescence. American student organizations, because of their pragmatic approach, have had a more difficult task surviving when struggles are not at a high pitch.

A general characteristic of student political activity is the rapidly changing focus of attention of the student activists, and the mercurial quality of student organizations. American students are not alone in losing interest in a specific issue or organization. In many countries, there has been a rather regular pattern of student political action, which rises and falls with changes in the political and educational situation in the society. Even militant mass student movements, such as the Zengakuren in Japan, are plagued by periods of student apathy. It is significant that the strongly Marxist Zengakuren has often shifted its tactics and stressed such issues as better student living conditions or reduced tram fares for students instead of militant struggle against the government.

The problems of continuity of organization and leadership which bother the American movement are duplicated in most nations which have an active student movement. In a number of the new nations, the active student movements which participated in various anti-colonialist revolutions practically disappeared following independence. These student movements functioned effectively in an atmosphere of struggle, but seemingly could not adjust to periods of political calm. Student leaders, often idealists committed to goals of rapid modernization, found it difficult to function under seemingly slow-moving regimes, and either quit politics in despair or turned to extreme radical opposition. The parallel between such behavior in developing areas and the growing alienation from adults and the liberal "power structure" which can be seen in much of the American student movement today seems striking.

The relative weakness of the American student movement as compared to those abroad undoubtedly reflects institutional differences. The variation between the system of examinations in the United States and those in other countries may, for example, have an important impact on student political developments. In the United States, students are examined regularly and must be fairly well prepared if they are to continue in the university. In many of the developing nations and parts of Europe, however, examinations take place at yearly intervals (or even less often), thus allowing considerable leeway for outside student activities. Student movements in India and Latin America have strongly resisted efforts to upgrade standards through regular stringent examinations. They have also insisted that students who fail should have the right to repeat tests, that no one be dropped for bad grades. It is interesting to note that some of the student political activists in the United States do indeed drop out of college in order to participate more fully in the movement. The full program of extracurricular activities not related to politics which is offered in most American universities also decreases student political participation. In many of the developing areas, politics is one of the few areas open to student participation, since there is little or no provision of facilities for non-political extracurricular activities.

There are some important differences in the larger social systems which affect the nature of the student movements in the United States and those in many of the developing nations. The image of the college student, for example, differs greatly from country to country. In many of the developing areas, the student is one of the key modernizing elements in the society, is part of a small educated elite, and is treated, if not as a member of the ruling class, at least, with considerable respect. In these countries, the individual student may have a feeling of importance and of potential or actual power in his society. Student manifestos are often taken seriously by government officials, and the student organizations expect to be given a serious hearing by the government. It would be inconceivable that the President of the United States would hold protracted discussions with the leaders of the National Student Association in order to convince them to support the government's plans for social development. Yet this is exactly what happened in the Ivory Coast last year, and while the students eventually agreed with the president because of the threat of an end to scholarship aid, everyone recognized the importance of the students.

Student populations in many of the developing countries tend to be small, and relatively homogeneous. Often there is only one major university, which is located in the nation's capital, thus making the mobilization of student protest relatively easy. Students often come from relatively similar social class backgrounds, and many will have received their secondary educations in a small number of prestigious schools, thus building up the cohesion of the student community. The situation in the United States, with the college population approaching six millions and with more than 2,000 institutions of widely disparate kinds, is not at all analogous to those in the developing areas. The fate of an individual American student is relatively unimportant, and even the largest student organization, such as the SDS, means very little given the size of the educational establishment. The size of the system also makes it difficult to organize coordinated activity. The fairly wide range of class backgrounds, educational interests, and motives of American students makes them a very difficult group to stimulate to social action. Moreover, the vocational emphasis of American higher education is much greater than in universities in most developing areas, which have patterned their educational systems after British or French elitists models.

In the developing countries, there is an intrinsic conflict between the university and the society, thereby creating a fertile ground for student political awareness and participation. The university, as one of the primary modernizing elements in largely traditional societies, necessarily finds itself opposed to other elements in its society, and must often fight to protect its values and orientation. Students are often involved in these conflicts, and are key protectors of the modern orientation of the university. During the Nkrumah regime in Ghana, much of the student opposition to the government was based on the commitment of the university and of the student population to the modern values of academic freedom and to an institutionalization of an independent judiciary, a competent bureaucracy, etc. In much of Latin America, the student movements have attacked the traditional oligarchic elements in the society for resisting economic and social modernization. In the developed nations, on the other hand, no such conflict exists. The university is a carrier of the traditions of the society, as well as a training agency for necessary technical skills. It is a participant in a continuing modernizing development, rather than in the vanguard of such development. University students are not called upon to protect the values of their institutions against societal encroachments. In most cases, they are merely asked to gain the qualifications necessary for a useful role in a technological society. Thus, the place of the university in the developing and the advanced societies differs substantially, and these contrasts have an important role in shaping student political involvement.

. . .

Many developing areas have highly articulated traditions of student participation in, and sometimes leadership of, political events. In Latin America, students have participated in political affairs for generations and are expected to do so. They have well-defined powers in the governing of universities. In many Asian and African countries, students were a leading force in the struggles for independence, and former student leaders often achieved political power in the post-independence governments. Since independence, the student role in many of these countries has diminished substantially, although governments still must take account of the student movement. Recent events in South Korea, Turkey, Japan, Indonesia, South Vietnam, and other countries graphically emphasize the importance of the students.

The United States is a sharp contrast to this picture of semi-legitimated student political activity. American students have never been particularly active politically, and they are not generally expected to actively participate in their society. Student organizations have not been important in any aspect of American life, except for the civil rights struggle. A substantial majority of the student population has never been involved in political activity. The new student left is essentially going against the major trends in American academic life. Despite recent widespread publicity student political activity still is regarded in negative terms by a majority of the students, as well as by many educators and the general public.

It can be seen that there are both differences and similarities between the American student movement, and student political activities in the developing areas. This brief discussion has served mainly to point to a few of the more obvious factors. Ironically, students in many of the developing nations recently have begun to look to the relatively small American student movement for inspiration. The success of the civil rights movement, the Berkeley revolt, and other events have been well publicized in many nations. There has been close communications between the American student "new left" and its counterparts in other nations.

CONCLUSION

It is clear that the student movement in the United States has played a significant role in the past few years in the civil rights struggle in the South, in focusing attention on problems of higher education through the Berkeley revolt, and in beginning the national foreign policy debate on Vietnam. Yet, the student movement has not succeeded in mobilizing a really significant segment of the student population, or in substantially influencing either its educational environment or the broader society. Some of the causes for this weakness have been presented in the contrast between the developing areas and the United States. Basically, in the United States, with its relatively stable social system and a fairly long tradition of political tranquility, radical social movements of any kind have had difficulty in establishing themselves. Many of the developing nations, however, face major social problems and are trying desperately to transform their societies, to modernize, and to industrialize. There is often real ambivalence about roles in rapidly changing societies. Major segments of the society may be impatient at the rate of change, or feel they are suffering from its consequences. In such an atmosphere, radical social movements have a greater opportunity to expand.

While the American student movement is small, and in the long run may be almost insignificant in terms of its direct impact on society, there is always the possibility that it may be a precursor to a larger left-wing movement in the United States. Students have often played a "vanguard" role in different societies and an increase in student activism has sometimes heralded social change. It is possible that the new student left of the mid-1960's may imply some changes in American society. On the other hand, it is much more likely that it is one of many unsuccessful attempts in the United States to create a radical movement in an essentially unfertile environment.

Metropolitan Anomie and the Crisis in Leadership

SCOTT GREER

Ideologists of both the left and the right have all too often appealed to the people's mistrust of the few at the top—whether the "business establishment" in the case of the left or the "liberal establishment" in the case of the new right in America—who have always run things, so it is said, to suit themselves. Although this model of monolithic, elite dominance may have once been true in this country, this selection brings considerable evidence to bear on the thesis that the modern metropolitan community is so complex that any such model which assumes the simple dominance of "the interests" is very misleading. On the contrary, the considered conclusions of most of the serious social scientists who have worked in this field since World War II are far better summed up in the following paragraph, taken from the very end of this selection:

"Let it be assumed that effective decision-making at the community level is the prerequisite for democratic procedures in the larger political system. Everywhere community leadership faces a common problem, . . . namely, the issue is not the manipulation of the citizenry by a small elite, but rather the inability of elites to create the conditions required for making decisions."

It is to be hoped that all the selections in this book will have contributed, in their various ways, to an increased understanding as to why Professor Janowitz, a distinguished sociologist and student of leadership, was forced to the conclusion quoted above. For the difficulties in making decisions in a more or less democratic way surely highlight the need for community—or a sense of trust as

Reprinted with permission of The Free Press from *The Emerging City: Myth and Reality* by Scott Greer. Copyright © 1962, by The Free Press of Glencoe, a division of The Macmillan Company. The footnotes have been omitted.

between neighbors, citizens, races, older and younger generations, employers and employees, and leaders and followers of all kinds. The crisis of leadership faced by our large-scale society today is, in other words, intimately related to the search for community in modern America.

THERE HAVE ALWAYS BEEN MANY AMERICANS WHO PREFER TO believe that power in the local community is tightly organized in the hands of a few persons who represent "the interests." Perhaps this is a rural survival, for in the small town there is some evidence of consistent domination by those who control land, credit, and wealth. Such an image can be easily transplanted to the city, where the mass media emphasize a few large-scale images connected with the polity, ignoring the supporting organizations and their dependence upon the citizens. The average urbanite, viewing these affairs from a great social distance, can easily believe that a small circle of the powerful exists and runs the city.

This image of the metropolitan area's power structure usually relies upon the assumption that local government is merely the executive committee of the bourgeoisie and the politicians hired hands of those who control the massive resources of the corporations. Floyd Hunter has documented such an image for Atlanta, Georgia, ending up with a list of a small number of people who are said to run things. Such studies are based upon "perceived influence" and they suffer from a curious solipsism. For, if the notion of monolithic power structure is diffused through the society, and if one approaches the study of power by asking people what they think occurs, he is very apt to document a myth—held sincerely and even fervently by his subjects, but quite likely to be as far from the truth as any other proposition about society upon which most people agree.

There is a touching naïveté in this faith, shared equally by left, right, and center. The ideologues of the left, confused and bemused by social transformations never posited in their theories, cling to the notion that *some* things do not change. The businessmen of main street have a vested interest in the image: it emphasizes their prestige and power and reinforces their own notions of who the first-class citizens are, and what interests are legitimate. The vulgarized radicalism that has permeated American thinking leads diverse people to find reassurance in a conspiracy theory of local government.

When, however, careful scholars investigate the way key *decisions* come about in the metropolis, they find neither the dominance of business interests nor the simple order assumed in the myth. Recent studies of New York, Philadelphia, Boston, St. Louis, Chicago, and Syracuse all present striking evidence that there is no simple structure, hierarchical and monolithic, deploying the power of the ruling classes and running the city (Kaufman and Sayre, Reichley, Baltzell, Norton Long, Long and Greer, Banfield, Banfield and Meyerson, Wilson, Freeman and associates). Instead, the businessmen are seen as limited in their influence, poorly organized and internally divided in their interests—frequently, in short, captives or pawns in a game where they do not hold the decisive advantage and frequently do not understand the play. Metropolitan politics, a continual interplay of other interests, has been given the felicitous name of "an ecology of games" by Norton Long. For the single pyramidal structure of control in the city, he substitutes a pluralistic political world where, like a continual game of musical chairs, the chief actors change positions as the issues revolve.

The myth of the economic ruling class makes two major assumptions about the metropolitan community in large-scale society. It assumes that there is a great commitment by businessmen to the fate of the local community, resting upon a great commitment of their corporate wealth and power. It also assumes that they have the instrumental ability to affect the local polity in the light of their corporate interests, to "call the shots" as the community agenda is formulated and acted upon.

Perhaps at one time, in the early decades of expanding scale, these assumptions held true. Perhaps, when the various large cities were all important headquarters of massive corporations, the latter were such citizens as elephants among chickens. Certainly today both assumptions can be questioned. Mills has pointed out the consequences of increasing scale for the corporation's commitment to the local area. Increasing scale means corporate merger, and the great and powerful corporate citizens in the community of yesterday are, today, branch plants of national organizations. The consequences, from the point of view of the career bureaucrats who now manage these plants, have been spelled out by Norton Long in detail; the effects of such changes upon the polity in a "satellite city" have been investigated by Schulze. Baltzell has demonstrated the diminishing concern of Philadelphia gentlemen for the local community, as their own interests focus more upon New York and Washington and they become part of a national upper class.

The manager of the branch plant is primarily a citizen in his national corporation, and his lodestar is company headquarters. To his own career, local affairs are relatively unimportant. His aim is to pursue the corporation's advantage (and thus his own) as quietly as possible, letting the sleeping community dogs lie. He makes a one-way gamble if he gets "involved" in local affairs—it can profit him little, and it can hurt him a great deal. His strategy is the limited one of protecting the company's public relations and trying to keep at least a consultative status and a veto on those issues that could cost the company dearly. And so his role is usually defined by headquarters. Proconsular in his position, each major commitment to the local community must be reviewed by his superior and every cent of his war chest accounted for. Powerful as he may be in the imaginations of local citizens, his power is usually the passive force of a bureaucratic instrument, part of a larger social machine.

In the corporation headquarters city matters may have another weight, for here the autonomy and the power coexist. But in the headquarters of a national or international organizational network, immediate local affairs usually appear trivial. In the light of the corporation's function, the chief advantage of *this* city, *this* community, may be no more than the residential preferences of the top staff and a relatively minute investment in a building or two. The geography of large-scale bureaucracy is quite different from that of the geography textbooks. Organizational space supersedes geographical space for most purposes.

So much for the real giants of American business and industry; they are, in large degree, neutral actors in the local community polity. However, there are other firms that are inevitably committed to a given city. The metropolitan newspapers are nontransferable assets, and their fate is linked to that of their city. So also are the local banks (particularly in states that forbid branch banking) and the closely related real-estate companies. Public utilities are earth-bound, their fortunes inextricably involved with those of the metropolitan community as a whole. Retail merchants also have, in plant and clientele, assets that have value in this city, but perhaps in no other. The civic leaders of Chicago or St. Louis, Boston, Los Angeles, or Cleveland, are drawn from the managerial and ownership ranks of these businesses (and such businesses are apt to be locally owned). They are committed: their liability is greater—they have nowhere else to go. They are, then, the chief corporate actors of business in the local community.

But there is a second assumption underpinning the classic myth of community control: the committed economic powers have the ability to call the tune for local government. Again, this may once have held, in smaller cities of a smaller-scale society. But in a society where the decisive actors of formal government are elected by the citizens, such political actors would have to share either a common normative system with voters and businessmen, or else have great freedom from the opinions of the voters and a great commitment to businessmen. The mechanisms assumed are usually (1) gross manipulation of votes and voters, insuring freedom from the electorate and its interests, and (2) the need for money from businessmen, for elections, bribery, and the personal income of politicians (for an extreme statement, see "Plunkitt of Tammany Hall").

These conditions certainly do not obtain in the contemporary metropolitan area. Neither the amateur governments of the suburbs nor the large-scale government of the central city can disregard the perceived interests of a majority with impunity. The increasing education, income, and occupational level that have affected all of the diverse populations of the city have forced an increasing emphasis upon issues of the community that are real to the residents. The absorption of the children of immigrants into the middle ranks of the familistic neighborhoods has weakened the power of the "ethnic name." Such devices as voting machines have made ballot-box stuffing increasingly dangerous. These changes in the nature of elections and the electorate have shifted the strategies of political victory from the simple disbursement of money to manipulation of the local branch of the national political party—for it is the party label that wins. As this occurs, the power of the businessman's campaign donation has shrunken proportionately. While bribery is undoubtedly still effective in some cases, it should always be remembered that the politician, like any organizational actor, usually will put the conditions for job security and progress in the job above everything else. Bribery by business would be defined as "selling out" to the enemy. In short, the businessman cannot often affect an official's political success one way or the other.

The weakness of the businessman in politics is also partly a result of the massive shift in residence within the governmentally bifurcated metropolis. The population that has moved outward has included the great majority of what was once the Republican basis of strength in the central city. The familistic, nonethnic, higher-rank residents have moved to the suburbs, leaving a pathetic remnant of Republican councilmen to represent the two-party system in most great American cities.

Along with the Republican voters, the leaders of the business community have gone to the suburbs. Equally important is the loss of the middle-level cadres of the middle class—the aspiring junior executives and young lawyers, the educated and politically inclined clubwomen, the small businessmen. These are the people who could constitute an effective organizational middle class for the electoral contests of the city. Their disappearance from the scene leaves those economic leaders who remain in the city (in the town houses and private streets of yesterday) far up in the organizational stratosphere, with no links to the mass of voters. And the latter are, increasingly, union members, ethnics, and confirmed Democrats.

The central city has become a one-party state, and the party is one that business leaders, as good Republicans, would find unattractive even if they were welcome in it. The issues of the central city polity—public housing, aid for the handicapped, slum clearance, improvements in race relations, aid to dependent children—are not the issues close to the heart of their national party. Nor are the solutions hit upon any more welcome; federal aid in massive quantities, increasing taxes upon property and business enterprise, subsidy of mass transit—such policies do not sit well with the ideologist of Main Street.

Yet this civic agenda and these solutions are inescapable conditions within which he must live, for his treasure and his home are separated by more than space; they are separated by political boundaries and social milieus. The owners of the great investments downtown are committed willy-nilly to the policies of the central city with respect to taxation, urban redevelopment, highway location, building-construction regulations —yet they are often unable to influence that polity. The classic dichotomy between wealth and numbers is accentuated by the political schizophrenia of the business elite; the issues that concern their basic occupational interests are settled in the central city's chambers of government and at the polls of the urban wards, while they are citizens of small suburban municipalities.

As citizens of the toy government in suburbia, they are indeed influential. Under the guise of a nonpartisan government, the municipalities in areas of high social rank are usually conservative. They stand pat with a definition of themselves as business operations controlled by a board of directors and its chairman, administered by an appointed manager. Such a government is remarkably congruent with the businessman's ordinary occupational milieu, and within the limited powers and electorate of the upper-class suburb he is an involved and participating citizen. It is a good solution to the problem of governing residential enclaves of homogeneous, nonethnic, middle-class Americans. The trouble is that this is not the business leader's major governmental problem in contemporary cities. His overweening problem is the concentration of his wealth in a "foreign country" ruled by the Democrats, and for this his "board of directors" government is no solution at all.

For the central city, large in scale, heterogeneous in population, diverse and conflicting in its interests, demands a polity that takes its nature into account. The norms of efficiency and economy (with their hidden assumptions about what is important) are subordinated to the need for growth, rescue operations, adjustment to change—in short, the reorganization of the community to fit the changing demands of the citizens. Large central cities mirror the conflicts and dilemmas of large-scale society in their politics.

The disappearance of the opposition, however, has had profound effects upon the control structure of the central city. In the security of its control the Democratic Party can choose the officials of the city government with great freedom, since a Republican victory is highly unlikely. The party, however, suffers some of the effects V. O. Key has spelled out for the Democratic Party in the South. That is, the true arena where office is won becomes the party primary, in which party discipline is continually exposed to dangerous onslaughts.

Ironically, victory has disorganized the central city Democratic machine in a way that adversity could never do. The lack of a common enemy has dissolved the discipline of battle. At the same time, the preconditions for "tight" control of the primaries are disappearing. Civil service and federal welfare agencies cut down the patronage that can be used to water the fields. The solid wards of the uneducated ethnics who will do as they are told, the "mattress wards" that can be bought, become a small minority of an electorate whose whole relation to politics shifts with its rising educational level and greater income. The primaries are threatened by the friends and neighbors vote, as in the one-party South.

This dissolution of the party is camouflaged by the continued importance of "Democrats" in the government of the city. But the armature of the party organization is, more and more, the official bureaucracy of government—the team of incumbents with its tremendous advantage in publicity—while the party clubs diminish in importance. They will continue to exercise some influence, as long as the forced communities of Negroes and other ethnics are major parts of the central city electorate, but their nature will change as these wards grow more concerned with their own particular interests. These interests are most tangibly served by the incumbents through appointments, ordinances, and the distribution of public works. The net result of the Democratic victory in the central city has been the strengthening of the incumbent officials and a merging of latent and manifest political leadership, of party roles and governmental roles.

In the newer metropolitan areas, such as the California cities, the result has been a sort of nonpartisanship among elected officials. There the bases of party control, in unlimited patronage and the massive votes of the segregated wards, have never been strong enough to sustain a real machine. The heritage of formal nonpartisanship has blurred party lines, and the central city has evolved a kind of rule based almost entirely upon the party of the incumbents. For these reasons such cities may be, not deviants, but forerunners of the future government in all of the larger central cities.

Whatever the process by which he is first elected, the central city mayor, through the continual dramatization of the mass media, develops a very great staying power. He becomes, to an appreciable degree, "above his party." His personal following then allows him a degree of autonomy from the party, which he can exploit to separate himself from the public images of crooked politics. (Thus, the anomalous situation in which the mayor of a great city renowned for corruption in local government can be considered innocent of that corruption.) The mayor, however, still has a very great control over the administrative branches in most city governments, and his logistic advantages permit him to dominate his party. The result is a tendency toward the coalescence of his role and that of party boss.

The mayor, however, does not act with unlimited freedom. Although he can press to the limits with formal and informal directives and vetoes, he can do so only at a price. This price varies by issue, for the corporate interests involved shift as the bone of contention changes, from an increase in taxes to a fair employment ordinance, from an urban renewal project to a new public hospital. But there will always be interested parties. They range from other publicly elected officials to parts of the Democratic Party organization, from a social segment of the voters, such as Negroes or Jews, to the chamber of commerce, from powerful members of the national party hierarchy to influential leaders of the local business community. In any case, the newspapers will mirror the struggle, sketch in the protagonists, report their speeches, and lay the basis for opinion formation. And, frequently, the newspapers themselves are key protagonists.

The mayor comes to stand, then, for the reconciliation of the diverse and conflicting interests of the city in a single polity. Standing above the factions in his public image (and frequently in fact) he is forced to consider the common interest of the city as a whole. Though each interest group can press without inhibition, his role is not that of an interest-group representative. He may even become, in many cases, an enemy of his own party organization, for his role in the functioning organization of the city is so demanding that he tends to sacrifice the tactical advantages of the party machine to the necessities of good administrative practice as he understands it. Sooner or later the central city mayor is apt to decide that "good government is good politics." And it is, for him. It allows him to rise above his party, to desert the boys in the back room, to capture the imaginations of the suburbanites as well as the heterogeneous denizens of the urban neighborhoods—to become a symbol of the metropolitan community.

His role places him astride the divided metropolitan area like a colossus; it is the major political position in the metropolitan community as a whole. In suburbs and central city alike, the large minority of the residents who perceive an area-wide leadership will concentrate their nominations upon political actors—and the chief actor is the mayor of the city. In the same way as city government in general, he acts on a large scale and he is a hero of the mass media. Furthermore, today he is everywhere concerned with the disjunction between his rights and his duties. So many of the central city's problems are inevitable concomitants of change originating far beyond its boundaries that he, who is responsible for them, is painfully aware of the consequences of the governmental dichotomy for the area as a whole. He is necessarily a "metropolitan citizen." (In the recent campaign for a metropolitan district government in St. Louis the mayor of the central city was the chief authority respected by the citizens, even in the suburbs. He was known and his opinion on the proposed change was known, by a majority of those who voted.) Of all the evidence that the metropolitan area is, in some sense, a single social and political community, this generalized importance of the central city's politics and particularly its mayor, is the most impressive.

Thus, local government in the metropolitan area does not approach the image of the monolithic power structure at many points. Instead of a pyramidal structure, controlled at the top by the representatives of economic interests, we find a pluralistic world of corporate citizens contending for power. The veto groups range from the corporation whose assets are captive to the polity of the central city, on one hand, to the Puerto Rican wards or the suburban municipalities on the other.

This contention occurs within a framework dominated by the political organization—and in the central city that organization is the local wing of the Democratic Party. But because of recent political transformations the governmental personnel are generally dominant. The team of the incumbents, especially the big city mayor, are the key actors. Among them, the heads of the giant bureaucracies loom large. They move consistently and continuously toward autonomy, security, and expansion. Fire, education, police, health, and other specialized agencies become organizational empires outlasting any given administration. Their professional commitments and relative freedom from party apparatus allow a genuine concern with universal norms. The mayor's autonomy allows him to concern himself also with the welfare of the city as a whole. The two kinds of actor, in combination, stand for political virtue and expertise. These attributes are frequently respected, in turn, by business representatives, who see in a "clean" and professional mayor only another executive like themselves.

Big business has few "trading cards" for the game of big city politics. It can exercise real power only at the top, for it lacks the troops to contend in the electoral domain. Its chief political force derives from (1) bargaining rights due to party control elsewhere, in the State House or in Washington; and (2) the potency of the newspapers, which are usually Republican in their ideology and which are big business in their own right. As distinguished from "power," businessmen have influence insofar as their opinion, as experts and as folk heroes of American middle-class society, matters to the mayor and his team. Evidence indicates that, in certain respects, it matters a great deal. For the big city mayor, emancipated from his machine allies, behaves much like a respectable, suburban, middle-class citizen.

In the multitudinous municipalities of suburbia, a power structure does frequently exist. But it is a structure very democratic in its nature. The social homogeneity of the citizens, their equality in social honor and resources, their common image of the local community—all these result in a self-selected sample that holds the offices of government. This oligarchy overemphasizes the role of businessmen, for their prestige is transferable to the political realm in a community that accepts the ethos of Main Street as definitive. They often produce a "clean" government, run by a manager, supported by a good government caucus party whose ward-heelers are members of the League of Women Voters.

Within these frameworks of control, the everyday business of governing a metropolis proceeds. In the central city the organizational subsegments of government are social machines organized as bureaucracies, governed by explicit norms and informed with professional codes. The public administrator and the jurisprudent, the specialist in police administration and the certified public accountant, are culture carriers who rationalize (and disenchant) the jungle of corruption and power that so fascinated Lord Bryce. For party conflict is substituted competition among the "different branches of the service," the lobbying of special interest groups and the struggle of party chieftains (who are usually elected officials) for the succession.

In the suburban municipalities the management-oriented administrator is also frequently dominant, as is the city manager of a small city. He works patiently within the circle of his amateur politicians, trying to educate them to the necessities of operating a going concern (which the municipality is) within a context of public responsibility and visibility (which a business firm is not). In towns without professional managers, the reason for their absence is usually anemia of the fisc; though some corruption occurs in such places, it is much more likely to be the incompetence of the officials that strikes the observer.

The sum of these arguments then, is this. No polity can embrace the total metropolis: too many legally autonomous structures are in being and there is always the dichotomy between central city and suburbia. Nor is a powerful, consistent, and continuous program of change likely in a central city. The mayor has strength, but chiefly to arbitrate among competing bureaucracies, business interests, ethnic minorities, and party organizations. Banfield describes Chicago's major issues for a two-year period; the majority resulted in stalemate and were tabled. Sayre and Kaufman show the city of New York as a mandarin bureaucracy, dominated by an irresponsible and conservative Board of Estimate. In short, the only dynamic that is consistent through time is that resulting from the continuous efforts of the "nonpolitical" civic bureaucracies to expand. In the process, services are provided within the limits of precedent. A minimal order is maintained. The past is the basis for extrapolation into a future where its rules and rules of thumb may or may not work.

Janowitz has put it succinctly. "Let it be assumed that effective decision-making at the community level is the prerequisite for democratic procedures in the larger political system. Everywhere community leadership faces a common problem . . . namely, the issue is not the manipulation of the citizenry by a small elite, but rather the inability of elites to create the conditions required for making decisions."

SELECTIVE BIBLIOGRAPHY

All the following references, except where noted to the contrary, are now available in paperback editions. Dates in parentheses after the titles of books refer to original publication dates so that the reader will know approximately when the book was written.

By far the best introduction to the classic sociological theory on community is contained in a just-published (hard-cover) volume entitled *The Sociological Tradition,* by Robert A. Nisbet (1966); in addition to being a creative analytical work in its own right, this book will also provide the student with the relevant citations to the classic literature of de Tocqueville, Durkheim, Simmel, Marx, and Weber. As an antidote to the classic literature, as well as Professor Nisbet's analysis of it, the student should read *The Secular City* (1965), by Harvey Cox. Professor Cox, a thorough student of both sociology and theology, is far less pessimistic about our modern world of secular social relations than were the classic theorists.

A selected list of the more recent theoretical literature on the modern problem of community would include the following: Eric Fromm, *Escape from Freedom* (1941), which brilliantly combines a Marxist and Freudian approach to the understanding of Nazi Germany; *The Lonely Crowd* (1950), by David Riesman, in collaboration with Rueul Denney and Nathan Glazer, is, of course, a modern classic; Sebastian De Grazia, *The Political Community: A Study in Anomie* (1948) and Robert A.

Nisbet, *Community and Power* (1953), both of which carry on the approaches to community cohesion first developed by the two great French theorists, Émile Durkheim and Alexis de Tocqueville. In many ways, Walter Lippmann's *A Preface to Morals* (1929) is still one of the best treatments of this subject, and his more recent book *The Public Philosophy* (1955) is also extremely useful.

The classic work on the problem of social mobility is still Pitirim A. Sorokin's brilliant book *Social Mobility* (1927), which is now available in paperback under the title *Social and Cultural Mobility.* The San Francisco longshoreman Eric Hoffer is truly an original thinker who has concentrated on the problem of social change and rootlessness; in his two books, *The True Believer* (1951) and *The Ordeal of Change* (1963), he develops the thesis that change makes misfits, and misfits become "true believers," who find a "new freedom—freedom to hate, bully, lie, torture, murder, and betray without shame and remorse."

A useful historical monograph for gaining an understanding of the transition generations of the 1880s through the New Deal is Richard Hofstadter, *The Age of Reform* (1955); part IV, from which we have quoted in the Introduction, is especially appropriate. For an understanding of the birth of modern social science in an age of change, there is nothing to compare with Beatrice Webb's autobiographical study *My Apprenticeship* (1926), now available in a Penguin edition. For insight into the relationship between status and community problems and the rise of the radical right in America, the best book is *The Radical Right* (1963), edited by Daniel Bell.

A multitude of community studies have been written by American sociologists, especially between the 1920s and the present. The best ones, from the point of view of this book, would include: Robert Lynd and Helen Lynd, *Middletown* (1929) and *Middletown in Transition* (1937). The Yankee City Series (1941–1961), by W. Lloyd Warner and his various associates, is best approached for the first time through an abridged, paperback edition by W. Lloyd Warner, *Yankee City* (1963). Allison Davis, B. B. Gardner, and M. R. Gardner, *Deep South* (1941) is an excellent study of a southern town by students of W. Lloyd Warner; Robert A. Dahl, *Who Governs* (1961) is a fine study of New Haven, from both a historical and an analytical point of view. Finally, Arthur J. Vidich and Joseph Bensman's *Small Town in Mass Society* (1960) is, from the point of view developed here, the best book of all; it should be read along with two excellent, theoretical and critical analyses of the classical community studies: Maurice R. Stein, *The Eclipse of Community* (1960) and Arthur J. Vidich, Joseph Bensman, and Maurice R. Stein, *Reflections on Community Studies* (1964). (As yet, the latter is unavailable in paperback.)

Since World War II, sociologists have turned their attention to the problem of suburbia. An excellent book to begin with is William M. Dobriner, *Class in Suburbia* (1963), from which the fourth essay in this book is taken; and William M. Dobriner (ed.), *The Suburban Community* (1958, hardcover only) provides a wide range of valuable insights. The first empirical study of the postwar, transient suburbanite is, of course, part VII of *The Organization Man* (1956), by William H. Whyte, Jr., only part of which is presented here. Although not a report on an American community, *Chrestwood Heights* (1956), by John R. Seeley, R. A. Sim, and E. W. Loosley, a study of an upper-class, Canadian suburb, provides insights into the life of the status-striving suburbanite which are equally applicable to our own society. This book might most profitably be read along with *The Exurbanites,* by A. C. Spectorsky (1958).

The search for community in the modern metropolis is the central theme of Jane Jacobs' *The Death and Life of Great American Cities* (1961), a portion of which appears here. The first empirical school of American sociology was born in the 1920s at the University of Chicago, under the inspiring leadership of Robert E. Park. Nineteen of the first thirty-five presidents of the American Sociological Society received their doctorates from Chicago. Park's central thesis was that community disorganization was a product of mobility and individualization. His students turned out a whole series of now classic works, among which the following are important here: Clifford R. Shaw, *The Jackroller* (1930); Robert Faris and Warren H. Dunham, *Mental Disorders in Urban Areas* (1939); E. V. Stonequist, *The Marginal Man* (1937); Frederick Thrasher, *The Gang* (1927); Louis Wirth, *The Ghetto* (1928); and Harvey Zorbaugh, *The Gold Coast and the Slum* (1929).

It is only since World War II that social scientists have begun to look at the corporation as a community rather than a purely economic association. This is one of the most important, and confusing, areas of modern society, as was noted in the Introduction. *The Organization Man* was the pioneer book. The work of A. A. Berle, Jr., is indispensable in this area, especially his little classic *The Twentieth-Century Capitalist Revolution* (1954). Here, the artists are often in the forefront of new insights: thus, J. P. Marquand's *The Late George Apley* (1937) was a portrait drawn with an upper-class community as the background, while his *Sincerely Willis Wade* (1955) is a study of the corporate community. Cameron Hawley's novel *Executive Suite* is an excellent analysis of the relationships between the family, the community, and the large corporation world.

The two novels mentioned above, as well as *Point of No Return* (1949) by J. P. Marquand are especially appropriate here. Marquand grew up in Newburyport, Massachusetts (Warner's "Yankee City"), and these three novels are excellent examples of the conflict between community and the "great society" in the twentieth century. Other novels might also be suggested as illustrations of our theme: Sinclair Lewis's *Babbitt* (1922) is, of course, the classic study of status-striving destroying the self; F. Scott Fitzgerald's *The Great Gatsby* (1925) is a tragic story of the rootless hero; Theodore Dreiser's *Sister Carrie* (1900), *The Financier* (1912), *The Titan* (1914), and *An American Tragedy* (1925) all center around the theme of status-striving in urban America eventually destroying the self. Finally, Marcia Davenport's *The Valley of Decision* (1943) is an excellent example of the rich gradually withdrawing from community and the source of their wealth.

The best collection of essays on the Berkeley Revolt of 1964 is *The Berkeley Student Revolt,* edited by Seymour Martin Lipset and Sheldon S. Wolin (1965). An interesting reaction to the Genovese case and an examination of the relation of law to community cohesion is to be found in *The Good Samaritan and the Law,* edited by James M. Ratcliffe (1966). The classic work on the need for community among Negroes, and especially on the need for leaders rather than status-seekers, is, of course, the late E. Franklin Frazier's *Black Bourgeoisie* (1957). For an understanding of modern youth and their quest for community and a meaning in life, see Kenneth Keniston, *The Uncommitted* (1964).

UNIVERSITY LIBRARY
NOTTINGHAM

71 72 73 12 11 10 9 8 7 6 5 4